Jen Bridge

Order this book online at www.trafford.com
or email orders@trafford.com

Most Trafford titles are also available at major online book retailers.

Printed in the United States of America.

ISBN: 978-1-4669-3334-7 (sc)
ISBN: 978-1-4669-3333-0 (e)

Trafford rev. 06/01/2012

 www.trafford.com

North America & international
toll-free: 1 888 232 4444 (USA & Canada)
phone: 250 383 6864 ♦ fax: 812 355 4082

CONTENTS

CHAPTER 1

"*A*m I adopted?" I asked. A silence seemed to go on forever—the answer seemed to hang in the air. "Well yes, actually" was the reply. My stomach turned over and over, was I going to be sick? All these weeks I had been thinking about this question and wanting to find the right moment to ask. That moment was here at last and I was feeling so sick. "Why, oh why, why couldn't you have been my real mother?" I said to Nora? "Does daddy know? When did all this happen?" Poor Nora, she must have felt overwhelmed by this young child asking so many questions that she could not fully answer. "Please don't tell daddy", "Why not" said Nora. Your daddy knows just as much as I do."

"But why am I adopted? Where is my mother? I want to know where she is. Doesn't she love me anymore?" "It is a very long story", said Nora, "It will take a long time. It is time to sleep now, so cuddle down and give me a kiss—Good night God bless."

I lay down in my comfy feather bed and snuggled into the covers. What would happen now, would Nora and Bill give me to someone else, I thought? What happens to adopted children? Who has my photographs of me as a baby? Has my mother thrown them out like she has me? And so, many questions ran through my head. How was I going to cope tomorrow?

When I woke up the next day, my bed was wet, oh dear, I thought, now she really will throw me out, because it is not right for a ten year old to wet the bed. When Nora appeared and I told her the bed was wet she kindly said "It doesn't matter, we can sort it out." This was very kind of her, but did it change anything? I felt so miserable. Would everyday things go on as before? Luckily it was good that daddy had gone to work so that I wouldn't have to face him, I felt so ashamed.

The next few days carried on as usual for everyone except me, I spent all the moments when I was not busy thinking about my earlier life and waiting for Nora to have time to explain to me what had happened to my mother and father. No one had mentioned my father, where was he?

CHAPTER 2

*O*ne day, later in the week, when Nora was not too busy she sat me down and began to tell me all she knew about my early beginnings.

She said it was a long story. My birth mother, Hilda, had a hard childhood, she herself did not know who her father was, as her mother, when working in service at a large country house, fell in love with the son of the house and became pregnant. She was at once dismissed and sent home in disgrace. She had no chance of seeing her boyfriend. Her extended family helped to bring up my mother (Hilda) until her mother eventually married a man called Kenneth. Hilda was then allowed to live with her mother and step father at the age of approximately 8 years of age. Ken was a bully of a man and sexually abused Hilda until she eventually ran away at the age of 18. Hilda met a married man who was not happy with his wife (how many times have we heard that statement!). They left their individual homes and went to Clacton-on-Sea where they spent the summer with each other. They ran a sweet stall on the sea-front during the summer months. When my mother Hilda, told her new partner (Stanley) that she was now pregnant, he could not cope and slunk back to his wife, leaving Hilda to fend for herself.

Hilda was by this time estranged from her family by her behaviour, so she was unable to return there. She managed to get a job working in a laundry until the time of my arrival. I have no details of how she was during my birth, but she has subsequently told me I weighed in at 9lbs.

After my birth Hilda found she could not support herself adequately, or even pay the bill for her confinement (there was no National Health Service in 1934). She forged her stepfather's name on the bills and hoped they would go away. Of course they did not and the law caught up with her, causing them to send her away for correction. Nora was not sure exactly what her punishment was, but she has hinted that she was in a workhouse type of place where she worked in a laundry and was badly treated. That meant that the Social Services of the time came and took me away from her and placed me with a foster mother. Hilda has since told me she was devastated when they "Took my baby away". She described how I looked so good in a pink knitted suit which she had knitted herself.

Sometime later, I am not sure when, I was transferred to a "Baby Farm". These were notoriously bad places for children. The description "Baby Farm", calls all sorts of ideas to mind, but I was reliably told that it was pretty awful for me. The good thing is that children below the age of three years have great difficulty remembering very many details of their lives. This was the same with me; I cannot remember anything about my life before I was adopted.

CHAPTER 3

When I was two and a half years old, I was taken to Nora and William's house for them to look after me temporarily, or "Until Hilda can get on her feet" my grandmother (Flo) told Nora.

Nora said she was cousin to my maternal grandmother, I was taught to call her Auntie Flo. When my grandmother told Nora about the plight of Hilda and myself, Nora became very upset that such horrid things could happen to a young child, especially when I was a distant relative of hers. Nora being the generous hearted woman she was, suggested that I come to stay with them for a short time until Hilda sorted things out. Nora and William had only one son of their own—Norman—who was at that time 20 years old and engaged to be married to Connie—also 20 years old.

So the day came for me to travel from Colchester (the place of the Baby Farm) with Hilda and my grandmother (Auntie Flo). Hilda has subsequently told me that she herself was told that I would be staying for a couple of days, then she would be back at her old house with her mother and step father to support her. This was not the case—as soon as I had been deposited with Nora and William, Hilda was turned away from her home by her mother and step-father to fend for herself again as best she could; another horrid blow for her.

Nora said that I travelled on the train from Colchester to High Wycombe, with changes of train at several stations on the way and had been given only one fruit bun to eat during the day. Nora told me I arrived, very dirty, dishevelled and scruffily dressed and obviously ravenously hungry and thirsty. My feet were poking out at the end of my shoes, because they were far too small for me. As soon as I saw boiled eggs, I wanted to eat straight away and didn't speak or look at anyone until I had finished the boiled egg and beautifully thinly cut bread and butter by William, I even asked for more. I apparently didn't seem at all fazed when Hilda and my grandmother left the house, in fact Nora said I didn't even wave goodbye.

As soon as they had left, Nora said she couldn't stand to look at me being so dirty and dishevelled; I had no more clothes to change into, so we got on the bus and went to the shops to kit me out in some new clothes. The next job was to get me in the bath and wash my hair about four times! After being dressed in a new nightdress they put me to bed on a small camp bed in their room. Nora said that I wanted the light out immediately after she had said goodnight. Apparently I slept like a log until about 7.00am. On waking I was extremely shy with Nora and William, but soon changed once there was food to eat!—Nothing changes then!

After breakfast it was time to explore the immediate vicinity. Nora's brother Bert and his wife Vi lived next door to her with their daughter Mary. Mary was the same age as myself and was very used to toddling into Nora's garden for a bit of fuss and sweets. The moment I set my eyes on this other little girl toddling into my space, I lifted a piece of wood and went to hit her on the head. Luckily for me, and Mary, Nora was close by and averted the near tragedy! I have no recollection of this event! For ever after Auntie Vi treated me with great caution and disdain!

Nora told me I was not able to speak very well and there began a time of teaching me to talk properly and behave as she would wish her own child to behave. I do remember retreating under a chair so that I wouldn't have to repeat words that others wanted me to; one word I remember was 'Palmolive', goodness knows why I needed to learn that one!

Nora found that my hair was infested with fleas and nits, and she went about the job of clearing them with great gusto! In fact one of my earliest memories is having my hair washed with Derbac Soap and being rinsed with vinegar at least two or three times a week. It was unusual in those days for anyone to have their hair washed or even bathe more than once a week, but you can bet that Nora made sure I was clean by getting out the tin bath, in front of the fire, most nights before I went to bed. We did have a proper bath upstairs, but no central heating, therefore it was warmer in front of the fire. Norman and Connie spent quite a bit of time teaching me to talk and taking me out on little trips with them. I can remember going out with them and thoroughly enjoying everything we did. We also had a small dog resident in the house, her name was Flossy and she took to me immediately and became a great pal of mine.

Soon after my arrival, Nora became very ill with kidney failure and very high blood pressure. She was confined to bed and the only significant memory I have of those days was when Nora turned over in her bed and my precious china doll fell onto the floor and smashed. She was a beautiful black china doll and Nora had bought for me and she had knitted her some clothes. One can imagine how I felt—much more upset about the doll than about Nora being ill! But I believe that is normal for a three and a half year old. Unbeknown to me, it must have been a difficult decision for Nora and William to keep me at their house, due to her continuing problem with raised blood pressure. I can only now appreciate the decision they made to carry on caring for me. Nora slowly improved, but never was fully fit for the rest of her life.

CHAPTER 4

$\mathcal{L}$ ife went on from that momentous day of my arrival to live with these two wonderful people. Three memorable things happened when I was five. First of these was the marriage of Connie and Norman. I was to be bridesmaid and I can remember the beautiful dress (Connie had made), it was a rust coloured velvet dress with tiny buttons all down the front, as it was to be a winter wedding. I used to go into Nora's bedroom and open the large wardrobe door and gaze upon the dress in awe. The problem that occurred was that Connie and Norman fell out with one another just one week before the wedding, so all the special arrangements were cancelled. I was devastated to hear a week later that they had got married after all, but in a Registry Office with only their parents present. I carried on gazing at the dress for weeks, until it mysteriously disappeared forever.

The second thing to happen was the start of World War II on the 3rd September 1939. Goodness me, what a fuss everyone made and to my mind nothing changed for quite a while. I was told that when the warning siren did sound I should go to the space under the stairs for safety. It was amazing how much trust everyone placed in this suggestion. Even my little desk was placed under the stairs so that I would not be bored and could carry on drawing or colouring or whatever I wanted. The desk was a great favourite of mine, it was painted pale blue and had a lid that lifted up and a space below to store my papers and books and pencils. The little chair that accompanied the desk was also pale blue. On the top of the desk was an ink well, which to my knowledge never once had any liquid ink in it at all. I used to play 'post offices' most of the time—I really liked the stamping kit which was included in the box. Wonder of wonders, on the day that war was declared, the siren wailed and wailed (I thought it a very strange noise, because it went on and on) and I was told to retreat to under the stairs! The amazing thing was that no one else went under the stairs, only me! After sitting there for some time, the 'all clear' siren was sounded. Nothing happened at all! This was how it went on for a very long time.

Food and clothing rationing came into being; everything we bought had to be accompanied with paper numbers that were cut out of a small booklet (called "The Ration Book") by the shop keeper. If there weren't enough little squares left we simply had to go without.

The third thing to happen was that I started school. It was lovely, all those children to play with, I couldn't contain my excitement. Mary and I were taken, together, to Totteridge Road Infants' School. We had to walk quite a little way, but that was part of the excitement. I remember meeting a few children, one of which became my life-long friend, and her name was Julie.

There was a big problem straight away, I could not write my name! I could copy everyone else's, but I seemed incapable of writing my own. If the class was asked to draw a picture, I copied Mary's or anyone else's that was close by. This caused quite a bit of consternation and many tears from me, because I didn't understand why I couldn't copy others. In the end I went home and practiced all day, most days, to write my name, in fact all my reading books of the day were covered with my name on all the pages! There seemed to be another problem, which was that at a special time designated for playing with any of the toys that were around the classroom, we were allowed to choose which toy we wished to play with. My choice was a "Woodwork Set", but unfortunately for me I didn't seem to understand that boy's toys were for boys and girls toys were for girls! This was pressed home to me in no uncertain manner. Many tears were shed again!

CHAPTER 5

*A*t the age of six and a half I began piano lessons. I enjoyed playing the little pieces from the lovely books that the piano teacher provided for us. I think Julie also started lessons; Mary was not interested. We had a very old piano which had candlesticks on the front of it and the white keys which were going very yellow in colour. I used to lovingly polish the piano most days. Connie could play the piano and when she and Norman visited some Sunday evenings, we used to have a sing-song around the piano; mostly singing hymns, but sometimes some community songs as well. I used to love to hear Connie play a piece of music called "Robin's Return". I would nestle into Norman's lap and we would all listen to the lovely music cascading from this old piano even if it was 'out of tune'.

I started going to Sunday School and loved singing all the hymns. I don't think I learnt anything about God, but just enjoyed being in His presence and feeling the reverence of a large church. I believe the church was a Church of England and was situated overlooking the railway line at the bottom end of our road.

The war progressed and my time under the stairs was stopped, I am not sure why. We became even more vulnerable, because if the siren sounded, and by now there was the occasional bomb dropped nearby, I used to climb up on to Nora's lap and cling to her feeling very scared. William by this time joined the ARP wardens, and every time the siren went he dressed up in his uniform and went off to help with any problems which might occur. Air Raid Precautions wardens were organised by the government of the day and run by local authorities to protect civilians from the danger of air-raids. Their main purpose was to patrol the streets during 'blackout' and ensure no light was visible. If they found a light they had to shout at the person responsible "Put that light out"! There were 1.4 million volunteer ARP wardens in Britain during the war. Part of William's uniform was a wide white belt with loops, one of the loops held what seemed to me to be an enormous chopper. I was very impressed, but I am not sure when or how he used the chopper! He also had a metal helmet on which was a large white W.

At school we were issued with a gas mask. This was kept in a small square cardboard box with string, making it possible to carry it over the shoulder. We had many times of practice at school in putting the thing on and taking it off and stowing it away in our small boxes. Luckily we never needed to use them for gas; the smell inside the gas mask was very odd, it also felt very claustrophobic. It was made of rubber and had a snout-like end which was made of shiny green metal with holes in to enable one to breath air from outside when wearing it. I used to wonder why the gas did not go in through these holes. As no one mentioned it to me, I gave up worrying. The boys in the class used them for all sorts of games and it didn't take long for the boxes to disintegrate! Some clever mothers made leather covers for the boxes and these looked very posh. One of my favourite songs at the time was "The White Cliffs of Dover", so I used to go around the house singing that song—"There'll be blue birds over . . . ."

Because we lived 27 miles from London we were part of the dropping off places for evacuees. The order went out that everyone (no excuses would be tolerated) must have an evacuee. The first one we had at our house was a very 'street wise' boy called Billy, of about 10 years of age. I remember he was very dirty and very naughty. Nora set about him straight away with the same vigour she had spent on me, but Billy was not to be clean or good! In no time at all he left to go back to London and we never heard from him again. I hope he survived the London blitz.

The next evacuee was a three year old Jewish boy. His mother came with him and stayed for a couple of weeks until he had settled down with us all. There was not much room in our little house, so Brian and I used to share a bed. Brian was very naughty at times and certainly very spoilt and precocious! He could tell if the aeroplane he could hear flying above was a "Jerry" and I was impressed with this boy. We spent many hours playing together, and although he was younger than I, we got on very well with each other. Sometime later on during the war, when things had died down a bit, his mother came for him and took him back to London. By this time there were no other evacuees to be housed, and our little family settled down again. After the war Nora and I went to visit Brian and his mum in London, but I found that Brian had grown into a very studious looking young man!

CHAPTER 6

When I was seven, Mary, Julie and I were transferred to a Junior School. This was a year earlier than normal, due to overcrowding at Totteridge Road School. The Junior School was an old Victorian School and seemed so large after our small Infant School. The first day we were there, we collected together in the large playground talking to each other, when suddenly the headmistress (called Miss Nichols) came and blew a whistle. All the children stopped what they were doing and listened. At that moment the boy next to me asked me if my toy watch which I had received from a Christmas cracker earlier in the year was real. I told him "No, of course not". Miss Nichols (the headmistress) heard me speak and pulled me out of the playground and stood me in the large hall in front of her room and said "You stay there until I come back". I was very frightened, but not sure what was to happen next. After the children had all been deposited in their classrooms, she returned to where I was standing and said "Come into my room". As soon as we were in there she picked up a long cane and asked me to put out my hand. She then proceeded to whack me across the palm of my hand at least four times. It hurt so much, and tears began to flow down my face. She said, "You were talking in the playground when you should not have been, you can now go to your classroom". This event had a devastating effect on me for the whole time I was at the school. I felt I had been unfairly treated, and this made me unhappy the whole time I was at this particular school. I was terrified of Miss Nichols whenever she came into a room where I was present. Miss Nichols had a nasty habit of creeping up and poking the children in the back, especially when they weren't aware of her presence, you can imagine how frightened everyone was when she was about. I don't think I ever told Nora or William about the events, because I felt so ashamed and felt it was my fault.

Mary, Julie and I joined the Brownies—what fun we had. We worked hard to earn badges and we learnt a great deal of useful practical skills. On the way home from brownies every week we would call at the fish and chip shop on our road and buy some "scrumps"—these were pieces of batter that had fallen off as the fish was fried—they were great, although I am sure they were not good for us, but never mind, we were extremely happy.

While at the Junior School we had air raid practices and spent many an afternoon in the cold, damp shelters which had been dug under the school playground. The smell of these shelters has never left me; it is a distinct smell, of which nothing else seems to be similar. We had to carry on working in the shelter if the siren went, although it was difficult for us to concentrate, because we were listening out for any bombs that might fall.

In 1942, children were sent out with paper bags to collect hips and haws from the wild roses in the fields. They told us that these fruits would produce Rose Hip Syrup which would provide children with all the vitamins that were missing from their daily diet. It was an exciting time; we tried to fill our papers bags before anyone else and great competition was produced.

We were taught to write letters to the soldiers, sailors and airmen who might be abroad, to keep them happy so they could win the war for us. We all had someone who was away in the war. I had two uncles who were in the Middle East countries during the war, so I wrote copious letters to them on flimsy airmail paper, in my best handwriting. Goodness knows if they appreciated them or not. In fact I know that one uncle did receive them, because I had a conversation with him when he was ninety years old. He was reminiscing as old folk do, and said he had many letters from me, but he never said whether he enjoyed them!

I hated school dinners at this school, because we were made to eat every morsel of food that had been put on the plate; never mind if we liked it or not. The memory I have is that the food was poorly cooked and tasteless. The meat was gristly and tough. This is when I formed my hatred of fat and gristle on meat, causing me to avoid meat at most meals, in case it was fat or gristly. The puddings were not much better, sponges were thick and heavy, pastry so hard that if you put a spoon into it was likely to split and shoot across the table, and there was a danger that the particular person across the table would eat your pudding! Sausages were gristly and undercooked; this has put me off sausages for ever! I used to have nightmares about food, Nora couldn't understand why. She always cooked lovely meals and also used to cook things she knew I would like. Some people would say I was spoilt by this, but I don't think it is spoiling people to give them food they like.

In school we sang many songs, such as "Volga Boat Song", "Danny Boy" and many others. We all enjoyed our time of singing. We also learnt to sew (at least the girls did!). I made a pair of knickers in beautiful pale blue lawn cotton. It took hours. When I tried to wear them, I found they didn't give when I bent down and I always split them at the back! You might say it was a waste of time to make something so unwearable but it wasn't really, because it taught me how to handle seams, etc. We were also taught how to mend sheets and other clothing. Children nowadays would laugh; they would throw things away if they tear. Even to this day I love mending things and still do if there is a need.

At the age of ten there was a raffle at school and the prize was a kitten. I remember the ticket was 2d and wonder of wonders, I won. When I arrived home, Nora and William were reluctant to keep the kitten, but were eventually persuaded by me that I would look after her. She was named "Ruffy" due to her type of fluffy fur which was black and white. She eventually grew to the ripe old age of 16 and was always a favourite family pet, loved by us all. When she grew into an adult cat she was wonderful at catching mice; we lived opposite a farm and when it was harvest time Ruffy used to disappear for days and come back with a bleeding nose and covered in straw and dust, she then slept for a long time.

Towards the end of the war Mary and I used to play in the nearby field and one day we heard what sounded like a plane, but didn't look like one that we knew. The engine suddenly stopped and the contraption sailed across the sky until it landed in the next field and blew up. That was our first sighting of a "Doodle Bug"! These horrid weapons had no pilot and made a droning noise which stopped 15 seconds before they fell to the ground and produced a powerful blast and destruction. They were called VI's; there were many more of these horrid things before the war ended.

CHAPTER 7

*A*t the age of ten I began to distrust the things Nora told me about her being my mother and William being my father. It was interesting to hear a conversation one day when I was out with Nora in the town shopping; the person she met and talked to said to Nora "Jen looks just like her mother". I began turning this over in my mind. I am still amazed today that someone would be stupid enough to think a 10 year old girl could not put two and two together and make four! I kept asking to see pictures of myself as a baby, but they said they didn't have any. I felt very uncomfortable about that.

I eventually plucked up courage to ask questions about whether I was adopted.

After Nora told me about my birth mother, I found that life for me was different. I found my thoughts about my mother, Hilda and my father, Stanley, were with me on and off every day. I could not get used to being different from other girls of my age. I tended to ask all my friends how they felt about their mothers and whether they felt loved. I was wetting the bed on odd occasions; Nora always forgave me and never grumbled about having to wash sheets all the time.

In 1944 a new School Act came out in an attempt to improve the education in Britain. The Act raised the school leaving age to 15 and Secondary Modern Schools were formed. It was about this time when the eleven plus exam became an important event at school. Mary was very clever and was expected to pass the eleven plus exam, whereas I was doubtful, due to my lack of concentration and being too talkative! On the day of the exam Mary and I set off for school having digested a good breakfast—"It is good for the brain," we were told. The exam was fun to me, I enjoyed it very much, I had no pressure on me to pass and I did my best within my ability. Needless to say I failed! Mary also failed! Mary's mum was sure it was my fault, for distracting her! Our fate was sealed; we that is, Mary, Julie and I would be going to a Secondary Modern School.

The war in Europe ended on 8th May 1945. All our streets had parties which were great fun with sandwiches and cakes provided by local mums and we sat at tables in the street, music played and we danced until darkness fell. Suddenly we had bananas and oranges, we had never seen them, at least not that we could remember. Food and clothing was still rationed, but more choice was appearing in the shops. A great excitement for us children was to have fresh fruit whenever we wanted.

Nora sat me down one day and asked me if I would like to be legally adopted by them, making me an equal with their own son as far as them being my mother and father. I considered this and agreed that probably it would be a good thing; after all it might make me feel more secure. Hilda had told Nora that she and her husband now desired me to live with them, but Nora said that as she hadn't bothered up to now, she should not be allowed to take me away from them. Some weeks later Nora, William and I went to the Juvenile Court in High Wycombe and stood before a magistrate and agreed to the adoption. In the court was Hilda, this threw me a little, as I really wanted to cuddle up to her and ask her why she had left me. I was asked who would I like to live with and, for a few seconds I hesitated, and then answered "Mum and Dad". My training as a "good" child made me hesitate and pretend I was quite alright with the situation. I reflected on the whole event for ages and was amazed that I didn't seem to feel any different.

I was still wetting the bed at night while I was asleep. I was very ashamed, but Nora told me it was OK. I am sure it wasn't OK, because in those days we slept on feather mattresses, and this must have caused an awful amount of work for her.

It came time to leave Brownies and go up to Guides. This was a great disappointment to me, the atmosphere in the guides was totally different from the Brownies and I for one hated it. It wasn't long before I left, and Mary and Julie left too.

Off we went to a Secondary Modern School. This school had only been built one year earlier and was so different from the last school. I was thrilled to bits with everything. Mary, Julie and I were put in the same class and remained together throughout the rest of our education. We were taught at a high standard and I am sure that if we had been subjected to GCSEs and A levels we would have passed them, because the standard of education was high.

One of the teachers who taught History will always be remembered by me. We used to call her "Stone Age Stella", although her name was Miss Martin. We were very impressed to find out she had a brother who was a "Beefeater" at the Tower of London. Looking back I realised she was absolutely perfect for raising an awareness in girls of the history of Great Britain. We started at the "Stone Age" and progressed during our four years a great way through history. Most of what she taught us has stayed somewhere at the back of our minds.

One day I was listening intently to Miss Martin and fiddling with my pencil case, which happened to be an old date box. Suddenly she shouted at me to concentrate, I was so startled I fell off my chair which folded up beneath me! Everyone laughed, except me!

We had to sew an apron in needlework before we could do any cookery. Depending upon the speed which the apron and hat was finished, the cooking instructions started. First we were taught how to wash our feet and dry them properly, then wash and dry our hair. Until we had learnt to keep clean we were not to be allowed to cook. Eventually we cooked, and cooked and cooked. We made stews, cakes, biscuits, pies, whole dinners, salads, fruit salads, custard, gravy, sauces, etc. I remember making a stew with vegetables and some sort of meat. When it was finished we took it home in a glass jar. Nora was a little suspicious, but in the end tasted a little and said "Not bad!" but I was left to eat it on my own!!

One of the memorable times at this school was an exchange visit with a school in Brighton. Thirty of their girls came to stay with us for two weeks, and then thirty of us went to stay with them in Brighton. The only difference being that the Brighton girls stayed in our school building, because it was new and had good amenities, but we were lucky enough to stay in a hotel on the sea front, this was probably due to the fact that their school building was very old. This was the first time away from Nora and William; I felt a little homesick, but not enough to spoil the whole event. It was a wonderful time and we all enjoyed every minute of it. We explored all the places around Brighton as well as the famous parts of Brighton, for example Brighton Pavilion. We had to write a journal while we were there and there was a competition for the best one. Surprise, surprise, I won first prize. I am sure it was because I had never been away from home before and found it so enjoyable that I won.

CHAPTER 8

*I*n August 1945, Nora and William decided to go on holiday to Bournemouth. Before the war they used to stay with a lady in Winton, Bournemouth for their regular holidays. When they wrote to this lady to see if they could resume their regular holidays, the lady wrote back to say that she had lost her husband during the war and didn't feel able to run a guest house any more, but was willing to give Nora and William another lady's name who lived in the same road and was just starting up with a guest house. Nora and William and I set off to Bournemouth in July and there I met Marjorie who was the daughter of Mr and Mrs Hammond who owned the guest house business in Winton, Bournemouth. Marjorie was the same age as me and therefore we had a lot in common. Whilst we were on holiday in Bournemouth V.J. (Victory over Japan) Day was announced on 8th August. Marjorie and I went into Bournemouth in the evening of V.J. DAY and found the American servicemen having a great time celebrating the end of the war. They were rolling Belisha beacon orange globes (these globes were on the top of black and white posts to help pedestrians cross roads) down the hill which led to the sea and they climbed lampposts and made a great deal of noise. The park in Bournemouth had lights all over for the first time since the war began. These lights were little pots painted in different colours with a lighted candle placed in each one and hung by string onto the bushes. Marjorie and I spent time blowing out the candles for fun. I was very sad to leave after a fortnight's holiday, but promised to write to Marjorie as often as I could. We hoped to return for more holidays in the future.

At twelve and a half, we were subjected to the thirteen plus exam which would send some of the children to the Technical College. I was reluctant to take this exam, because I was so happy at the school I did not want to move. Mary failed again! Therefore her fate was sealed; she had to stay with us. I passed! "There is no way I will go to that school", I declared.

Sport was a favourite of mine, although I could not say the same for Mary or Julie. I loved hurdles and long jump, but I especially enjoyed and loved netball. I became very good at it and was chosen to play for High Wycombe and also to play for the county team of Bucks. There was a problem at times because the netball tournaments were on Saturday mornings and so was my piano lesson—Nora would not budge, I had to attend the piano lesson most of the times and lost my place in the school team many times. In the winter we played hockey; this was in the games lesson and one day I managed to knock out Julie as I passed her. She recovered well, but I was in trouble for raising my stick too high. After that I wasn't keen on hockey in case I repeated by accident a similar event.

When we were in the last year at school we all had to spend a week in turn in the small flat attached to the cookery room. Three girls were expected to stay together in the flat (only during school day) and keep it clean and tidy and bath the baby (a doll). We had to cook a three course meal every day and invite two of the teachers. It was hard work, but very enjoyable.

In the last two years at this school, the children were sorted out into three different classes. One class was called Commercial, and prepared the girls to achieve skills to work in offices. The next class was called Housecraft, this prepared girls to work in jobs where skills for housekeeping were needed, and it also equipped the girls for marriage and motherhood. The third class was called "Rural". To us girls this was the dunces' class! Not so, it was designed for girls who would work on farms, gardens, shops selling garden ware, etc. Secretly I would have liked to spend some time in this class, but what would my colleagues have thought of me?

I had decided that I wanted to be a nurse. Nora had decided something else! She wanted me to be a Civil Servant (her brother Charles was a Civil Servant) and she didn't want me to work too hard physically. Nora said nurses in those days did a tremendous amount of "Washing and cleaning and scrubbing floors and worked long hours". Needless to say, I went into the "Commercial Class", so did Mary and Julie!

We had a great English Literature teacher, Miss Willet, who introduced us to Shakespeare and other authors. Every term she directed a play of some sort and we were all encouraged to take part. I remember only one of these plays and to this day I cannot remember the title. I had the part of a very, very fat King's mother, and Julie had the part of one of the crowd who shouted out "The King is fat, but look at that, it is the King's Mama!" Perhaps I should be on the stage, I thought, for many months following this play, because it opened up new ideas in my mind, which never came to fruition!

Because I could play the piano a little I joined a group of girls who could be trusted to play the piano for the entrance and departure of the girls at assembly. Sometimes I played pieces with other girls (duets). I am sure I played many wrong notes, but it didn't seem to stop me being part of this little group. By then I had decided that piano lessons were not for me, as I could not abide all the practice that was needed. Good job I could sight read fairly well and get by most of the time. I was not to be a concert pianist then, I decided.

One of our lessons was swimming and the only pool in High Wycombe was at the other end of the town in a field called "The Rec", of course it was an open air pool and the water was not only very cold, but as the water was filtered from a river, there were small creatures floating about in the water. One hoped not to swallow too many, although our minds were taken off this and concentrated on keeping as warm as possible in freezing conditions. I think I learned to swim so that I could keep warm.

During my school years Nora and William and I returned regularly to Bournemouth to stay with Mr and Mrs Hammond and of course, Marjorie. Marjorie and I shared many happy times during our school years. One year her school had not broken up for the holidays when we arrived, so we were both disappointed that she wasn't around to go out each day with us. The school that she attended went to Brockenhurst to see a production of Midsummer Night's Dream by Shakespeare and I was invited by her teachers to accompany them providing I borrowed a spare school uniform for the day. I remember the day well; it was so enjoyable.

CHAPTER 9

*W*e were very lucky that William owned a car, which was very unusual in those days for working class people. He said he bought it so that Nora could get out and about, because she could not walk very far due to her poor health. This meant that we were often out for trips around the area. One of the trips I remember was to a place called Brill which is in North Buckinghamshire. This was apparently where William was born and was brought up on a farm. When we visited it was like turning the clocks back to the 'dark ages' because the people who lived there had not moved on socially, they did not have any 'mod cons'. The toilet was a bucket under a wooden seat in the back yard—ugh, I hated it!

We also frequently visited a place called Burnham Beeches. At this place there were some magnificent beech trees and whatever time of the year we visited they were beautiful. During our time at Sunday School we were often taken to Burnham Beeches for our annual Sunday School Treat. We roamed the forest of trees, played organised games in a field and finally had tea seated at trestle tables laden with bread and jam and cakes. We all thought it was wonderful to go there for a day. Eventually an outdoor swimming pool was built so visits were more frequent to allow us to swim in the freezing cold water!

For a few weekends one summer we went to a farm in Little Marlow where my mother Hilda was living with her husband and six children. This was a great surprise to me to find these children. Every time we visited this family, Nora gave out sweets for the children and a piece of ham for them all or something similar. When I asked her why she did this, Nora replied that the family were extremely poor and had borrowed some money from Nora and William, and this way she could be sure that Hilda paid the money back each week. I was thrilled to be able to see Hilda, but quite disappointed with how I felt, in fact I did not have any feelings for her at all. I was more interested in her family of children. Nora was quite upset that I didn't gel with Hilda. I don't remember Hilda speaking to me at all.

William's car was kept in a field just across the road from our house, and William taught me to drive the car around the field and put the car into the garage. He was very brave to do this, because I rewarded him many times by taking off the front bumper as I drove into the garage. His language was not too good after these events, but it did not stop him from letting me have a go. He said he wanted me to learn to drive so that I could take Nora out shopping sometimes when he was at work. Of course I could not drive on the road until I was seventeen and able to get a provisional licence.

William had a sister called Lily, who had married late in life a man called Percy, they lived in Witney, Oxfordshire and Percy kept a butchers shop. Percy had a son called Jim who I found difficult to understand due to his strong Oxfordshire accent. Lily often invited her nieces to go to stay with her, and I enjoyed some visits from time to time at the butchers shop. It was interesting to watch Percy skin a rabbit; cut up the meat into portions, etc. He even let me feed into a machine some meat which came out as sausages! It was a very old house and shop and had an outside toilet with a wooden seat. I was so reluctant to go to the toilet when staying there, that I became very constipated by the time I reached home again!

Julie had joined "The Odeon Girls' Choir" and encouraged me to join her in this. I was auditioned and managed to get into the front row (I was too short for the back rows!). The local Odeon Cinema had decided that a girls' choir could sing at some of the Saturday Morning Matinees. These matinees were really popular; we could see all the cartoons and weekly serials about great heroes. The only problem was that some children did shout and talk all the way through these films which made it very difficult to hear the words. No one seemed to worry at all if the children made any noise, as long as everyone was in there and paid for their seat. I cannot remember how much we paid, but it was very cheap.

The Odeon Girls' Choir was entered into a countrywide competition every Christmas time and we won the title for four years running. We were taken to the Gaumont Cinema in London for a lunch and party and presented with silver medals for our achievement. It was all great fun. At home I used to sing in the bathroom with the door shut; mostly Deanna Durbin's songs. I began to think I was as good as Deanna Durbin and might become a famous singer in my own right! I enjoyed singing very much and learnt an awful amount about how to sing in a choir, which is vastly different from singing alone. Our conductor was called Mr Jones and he was a strict task master. He used to go around whilst we were singing and listen to each individual, and if they were singing out of tune he shouted at them "You can get out!" I am sure this is not the right way to behave, but it was the way in which we became better and better.

I did not tell Nora and William that I had applied to a college in nearby Slough for a place on a pre-nursing course. Unfortunately I did get a place and this brought the whole thing to a head. "No way", said Nora, "You are going to be a Civil Servant and that is the end of the matter". So that was the end of my ambitions to be a nurse (for the time being anyway).

CHAPTER 10

$\mathcal{M}$ary, Julie, Julie's cousin Janet and I were entered into the Civil Service exam, without which you could not become a Civil Servant at that time. We went up to London on the train to Caxton House and sat the exam; this was an exciting trip for us. After weeks of waiting we were all four told we had passed. We were then allocated to different offices in London. Julie was off to Ministry of Pensions, Mary to Ministry of Civil Aviation, Janet to Ministry of Agriculture and Fisheries (Min of Ag. and Fish we called it) and I was allocated to the Colonial Office. That was the time when Great Britain had a great number of colonies! You can imagine what great excitement this caused. Our parents were all extremely pleased with our success, as were our teachers.

The Odeon Girls' Choir changed their name and became The High Wycombe Girls' Choir. We had many concerts all over the borough and even outside. This was the time when the Luton Girls' Choir became famous and was singing on the radio very often, and we hoped we were as good as them. I was still spending many hours in the bathroom (acoustics were good there) singing Deanna Durbin songs and feeling as if I were really her. "Can't Help Singing" was my favourite song. Perhaps I was going to be a professional singer!

At one weekend Nora invited Valerie—one of my half-sisters to come and stay. At first I was very shy and withdrawn, but as the weekend went on we both began to enjoy each other's company. After this successful weekend, Valerie came frequently. Some of my friends said we looked very much alike. I was not sure if I wanted to look like her!

When we had passed our fifteenth birthday the time came for our education to stop, at least as we had known it so far. We were encouraged to attend evening classes by our teachers, but it turned out that travelling to London every day on the steam train took so much time out of our day; we were far too exhausted to do anything by the time we had returned home. William used to give me a lift to the station in his lorry (sitting on a clean sack specially saved for me) which he used for his job, at 7.10am. The train left at 7.15am and arrived in London at approximately 8.20am. The train seemed to stop at every station on the 27 mile journey and we met and enjoyed the company of many people over the next 18 months. When I arrived at Marylebone station I had to journey on the underground to Westminster, because the Colonial Office was situated in Great Smith Street at the back of Westminster Abbey. The others' journeys were shorter than mine and they were in various other sites in London.

Because we were all under the age of 16 years, the rule at that time in the Civil Service was that we be trained by them in typing and shorthand and one day per week we would have to attend a college somewhere. Luckily for us Julie and I were to attend Kingsway College in London on each Friday until we became sixteen; I am not sure where Mary and Janet attended. Julie and I thoroughly enjoyed our days together and I am afraid we learnt absolutely nothing at the college. The standard of education we had been used to was much better than this education, and therefore we had done almost everything they offered to teach us. The only memorable thing about the days was that the first lesson was at the YWCA swimming pool where we were taught to swim. Well, I was, but Julie never did succeed. We had many laughs when Julie tried so hard to keep on the surface of the water, but failed every time they let go of her. I won a bronze medallion for life saving in this pool. Nora even managed a visit to London to see me perform in the pool on a special open day. This was a great feat of courage for her, because by this time she was not in the best of health. And although I was only fifteen and a half, I appreciated her efforts to support me. I felt she was truly a proper mother to me.

The Civil Service training school was a room over Burton's Shop at Tottenham Court Road. I learnt to type quite quickly, but shorthand sent me off my head! I even dreamt in shorthand. I used to go to church on Sunday evenings and take the sermon down in shorthand for practice. In the end I refused to do shorthand at all and felt much better just as a typist. In the front of the class was a huge picture of the keys on which we were supposed to keep our eyes as we typed the simplest text to tunes which were played in strict time. The favourite tunes were records of Victor Sylvester dance tunes and these were used due to the strict tempo of the music! As we progressed with our typing skills we were moved farther and farther back in the class, until eventually one was situated on the back row and soon after this we were ready to start actual work in our individual offices that we had been allocated to.

When we were at this training school we stopped for morning break and had cocoa—no coffee then! I met a man called Mr Quinn, and fell instantly in love! He was injured during the war and was at the school to be retrained for a fairly easy non-physical job. He must have been at least 35 years old, but that didn't put me off. Every day on the train I knitted him some socks as a present to show my love for him.

The socks had a very difficult "Fair-isle" pattern, a bit like "Golf Socks" and I slaved for hours to finish them. When they were completed they were so tight I could hardly put my hand in, let alone a leg and foot! I had pulled the wool too tight at the back of the work, and so ended the socks! Mr Quinn decided he loved someone else and so I was distraught for a few weeks, but eventually never gave him another thought.

CHAPTER 11

The day came for me to start at the Colonial Office. My goodness, what a lot of typewriters there were in one room. Once I had been allocated one, I was told that was where I was to sit and I was responsible for the state of my typewriter. It didn't take me any time at all to work out how to repair simple breakages on my own and soon others were asking me to mend theirs. I wouldn't want you to think that I was an expert on typewriters, but I have always liked tinkering around with mechanical things but I could only repair the simplest tasks. Perhaps I would have been more proficient in these repairs if I had been allowed as a young child to play with the 'woodwork set'!

The amount of work coming into this office never seemed to let up, as fast as we cleared the storage places they were filled up again when we were not looking. There was a supervisor of this typing pool called Miss Cook who was very small and had a serious limp. She frightened the living daylights out of me. Sometimes I would be called into her little office to check all the work in the afternoons, which was a nightmare as I used to feel so sleepy while reading everything!

We worked five and a half days per week, starting at 9.00am and finishing at 5.00pm and Saturdays finishing at

1.00pm. The starting salary was £2 7s 6d. per week out of which had to come the season ticket for the train to London, the underground fares, lunches, payment to our families for board and the rest was our 'spends' as you can imagine, there was only a little left on which to indulge a teenage girl's fantasies.

I made friends with many of the girls in the typing pool at the Colonial Office, especially one friend called Jackie, who later became my bridesmaid. We spent our lunch hours in the Army and Navy Stores listening to records (we had no record players at home!), my favourite records being "The Nun's Chorus" and a song called "The Life of Little Jimmy". Sometimes we would spend our lunch hour in Westminster Abbey, where we would eat our sandwiches. Nearby was an old indoor swimming pool and we used to go there, especially in the winter because it was so warm, either during lunch hour or after work. Mary, Julie and Janet always seemed to manage to catch the 5.15pm train from Marylebone to High Wycombe, but because of the distance of the office from Marylebone, I could only manage to catch the 5.35pm. Travelling on the underground was horrendous; everyone ran everywhere, up and down the escalators and through the stations to change to a different line. The trains were extremely crowded and one had to push hard to squeeze just inside the doors as the guard used to say "Mind the doors". One day Julie ran so fast her shoe fell off and I picked it up and suggested she run without it! We always laugh about the incident whenever we see each other. All this activity certainly took its toll of my health and I was constantly in trouble with sinusitis. Eventually I applied for a transfer to High Wycombe to one of the government offices there.

CHAPTER 12

The office to which I was allocated was The District Valuer's Office, Inland Revenue in the centre of High Wycombe. Although the work was not as hard, I did not settle very well. The only good thing about this change was that I had more time and did not have to travel on smelly, dirty steam trains every day. I complained to the CO that I did not have enough work to do, so he gave me the switchboard to cope with as well as the typing. I was much happier with this situation.

I had always wanted a bike, so with my first week's wages I went to the local Curry's shop and chose a green Raleigh racing bike with dropped handlebars; a hire purchase agreement was set up and every week after that day I went to Curry's to pay the next instalment. The bike was wonderful, it was the very first purchase of my own that I had ever made. Nora and Bill were not sure about the hire purchase, but I wanted to show them that they could trust me. It took two years to pay the whole amount for the bike, and I was so proud of all my efforts. I loved riding the bike and kept it very clean. There was no garage to keep it in but Nora allowed me to park it in the hall just inside the front door, provided I had cleaned the wheels!

I was at last out on the roads with my L plate learning to drive, and was lucky enough to fail my first test! The reason I was lucky was that the examiner said he would like to give me some driving lessons. At this point I can hear people saying he must have had an ulterior motive, but no, he was serious and took me out for a few times and taught me so much. William had never had a test in his life and didn't understand what was needed for the test. Eventually I was tested again by a completely different man and passed with flying colours. When he asked who taught me and I replied "My father", he said "He must be a good driver and teacher". I kept very quiet about the whole thing because I did not want to get the previous examiner who taught me into any trouble.

I met a girl called Mary who loved horse riding and she encouraged me to go riding as often as I could afford to. I really enjoyed the horses and attended many 'regattas' but only for a ride, not to compete, I never reached that standard. We would ride in a group around the Marlow area for a whole afternoon, I loved it.

About this time I met a boy called Alan who was very keen to go out with me. His family attended the local Salvation Army Citadel in Wycombe. His mother was a 'songster'. Alan played a cornet in the band. Needless to say I attended quite a few services at the Citadel and enjoyed them. Connie and Norman both teased me about becoming a 'songster' and wearing a 'bonnet'. I eventually realised that there were better boys than Alan and told him I didn't want to see him again. His reaction was quite violent, he said he would get a gun and shoot me! Some weeks later when I should have been riding with Mary she was stopped in a field by Alan who was wielding what looked like a gun and asked where I was. Mary said she was quite scared, but told him to "get lost". I felt very anxious for a few weeks until eventually I forgot about him and actually never saw him again.

The next boy-friend I had was also called Alan. He was totally different from the first Alan. We went out and about together for a year or so, until I realised I wasn't happy with him. He was sensible and did not react badly when I said "It is finished".

Paul was the next boy-friend, he was extremely tall. He lived at Holmer Green, where Connie and Norman lived. We went around together for a while until again I felt he was not the one for me.

I was lucky enough to be able to ride my bicycle to work and I remember one morning (1st January) I rode down the road in which I lived and turned into the main London Road, unfortunately not noticing that there was ice on the road and the bicycle slid sideways and I came off. My chin hit the ground and split open, there was blood everywhere. An ambulance was called and I ended up with stitches across the bottom of my chin for a week. Incidentally I had half a dozen eggs in my saddle bag which did not even break—amazing!

During my teenage years I joined a youth club with Julie and Mary and we had a great time playing table tennis and talking to boys, etc. Julie and I had many 'boy-friends', none of them very serious. Mary unfortunately did not have 'boy-friends', she said she wasn't interested. Julie had joined Newland Methodist Church where she and her mother sang in the choir and Julie encouraged me to join with her. By this time the girls' choir had turned into Chiltern Ladies Choir, and we still belonged. It was at the Methodist Church that I began to listen and know all about God. There was a very good Sunday afternoon group of young people who joined together to talk about any subject that interested them and the leader was a lovely man called Mr Cant. Mr Cant involved all of us and encouraged us all to lead the group from time to time. One of the things he told us I will always remember, that when one was the speaker, one must always notice the time and keep to it and to your subject.

I enrolled for singing lessons and elocution lessons, and found out how much I did not know about singing or speaking! Julie and I began singing duets together and were invited to all the local churches to sing at various events, such as Women's Meetings, Special Sunday events and the like. We both enjoyed singing together.

CHAPTER 13

One Saturday evening Julie and I went to a Methodist Youth Squash—this was an arrangement once a month at one of the free churches in High Wycombe for any of the young people who wished to go. Games were played, quizzes arranged, and the evenings always finished with a very short service. Julie and I needed a boy-friend each to take to the looming Christmas party of the Ladies Choir as we were both at that time without a boy-friend. I had my eye on a lad who was Irish; I fell in love with his accent. Julie had her eye on another lad from High Wycombe. Later in the evening we found that Julie's lad said his father was very ill and he couldn't go anywhere at the moment and mine was already tied up with another girl across the other side of the room. What were we to do? Just at that moment a strange man came up to me and asked if he could take me home. I was totally amazed, because I had no idea that he was even there that evening. So I turned to him and said "Yes, if you like, but can you please take Julie home as well, because we are together?" He kindly agreed and that turned out to be the beginning of my courtship with my future husband, Len.

I accompanied Len to his Methodist Church sometimes and later became a member of their YPF (Young People's

Fellowship). This was my introduction to my acceptance of Jesus as my Saviour. We went on a trip to London with the YPF to hear and see Billy Graham preach. What an experience that was, with thousands of voices singing "How great thou art".

Len had two sisters and three brothers and lived at the opposite end of High Wycombe from myself. He was the eldest boy and second in the six children. All the boys were courting at the same time and it became quite a competition as to who would be able to get the front room at Len's house! I thoroughly enjoyed being part of a huge family; at least it seemed huge to me. Every Sunday we went to tea at Len's house and his mother coped admirably with whosoever arrived, and she never knew how many that would be! Norah and William were very happy that I was accompanied by Len, as they knew of his family and approved. Christmas at Len's house was wonderful, we all played many games and it was surprising how competitive Len's siblings were, but they never fell out with one another.

Eventually we became engaged and after a very short engagement we were married at Westbourne Street Methodist Church, High Wycombe on 3rd April 1954. Len's brother Adam was the 'best man' and Julie and my friend Jackie from London were the bridesmaids. Our brother-in-law Fred played the organ and a friend of Len's sang a duet with Harold Brown, our singing teacher. We spent our honeymoon at Bournemouth in a small hotel. At this hotel the family who owned it were very friendly and had a small boy called Charles. Len and I loved this little boy and said "If we have a son we will call him Charles"!

On the eve of our wedding, who should arrive at our house, but Hilda? I was so shocked I was speechless. She said she had heard we were getting married and wanted to bring a present; it was a set of glasses. I dutifully said thank you and felt so uncomfortable and unable to say anything else. Because Len and I were going to the church we caught the same bus as Hilda when she left to go home. She commented on the flowers I had with me, to decorate the church, and said "Those Irises are lovely, they are my favourite flowers and that's why I named you Iris". I was still speechless, but thoughts of hatred ran through my mind, because I did not like the name Iris, so also did not like the flowers and don't to this day. When I first arrived at Nora and William's house my first name was Iris and second name Jen. When I was legally adopted the names were turned round, which pleased me. I wanted to ask her there and then "Why did you give me away?" Luckily the bus stopped at our stop and we got off. I hoped I would not have to see her again.

We moved into Nora and William's front rooms— bedroom and lounge—and shared the kitchen and bathroom. We paid a rent for these rooms and tried hard to fit into their lives without disturbing them. After a few months we felt it would be better if we had something on our own. Len and I decided we had just about enough money to put down a deposit on a new house near Nora and William. The house was semi-detached (with garage space) built by Taylor Woodrow and would cost £1,895. It was part of a very large estate, in fact built on the field where Mary and I used to play as young girls. Len's sister Joyce and her husband Fred and their adopted son John decided to buy the other half of our semi-detached house.

Most days we would take our dog Paddy for a walk up the field to look at the state of our house. We took some pictures of the house at various stages and felt very excited that it would soon be ready for us. At this time we found out that I was pregnant and we were concerned that the house might not be ready in time for us as a family to move in.

I was still working at the District Valuer's Office when I was pregnant, until one day Len and I went to pictures and found the film ran on after 10.00pm, meaning we would have to run to catch the last bus home. We did not think about my being pregnant, but only about catching the bus. The next day I found I was losing some blood and I spoke to the doctor to enquire whether this was normal. He said he would visit me immediately, so as I was at work at this moment, I had to rush home as fast as I could so that I could be in bed when the doctor arrived! Not a very sensible thing to do, I suppose. The doctor told us that I was having contractions and as I was only about six months pregnant, this was not good. I would have to stay in bed and rest for at least six weeks. Goodness, I did get bored. People were very kind and sent me magazines and books, but I found this time very hard. The doctor said that I would have to leave work, so I duly resigned my Civil Service job reluctantly.

The baby was due on 4th January 1955, and we were presented with the key to our new house on that day. The decision to move in was postponed, so that I should have the baby first. Carol Susan was born at The Maternity Home at 4.30am on 16th January 1955 weighing 7lbs 14oz. Both Len and I and of course Nora and William were 'over the moon'. The birth was said to be 'normal' but I had other thoughts about that! There were so many stitches that felt I was sitting on a hedgehog! Len came to visit on the first night and when it was the end of visiting hour he had to have a piece of paper with his surname on to show the midwife through the glass of the nursery on the way out; he wasn't allowed to touch the baby. When he came to see me the next night we were discussing the baby and it was obvious that it wasn't Carol that he had seen the previous evening, but someone else's baby!

At that time people who had babies were kept in bed for many days and the baby was whisked away to a nursery so that cross-infection could be a kept to a minimum. I made up my mind that I would never have another baby! When eventually we came home from the nursing home to Norah and William's house, we had many visitors, family and friends and neighbours wanting to see this new baby. Adjusting to feeding, washing, cooking and general living, took some efforts on my part, my hormones were all over the place and I was glad that Norah was there to give me a helping hand. I never once thought of Hilda.

CHAPTER 14

*E*ventually when Carol was six weeks old we moved into our new house. The weather was very cold, so was the house. There was no central heating, only a coal fire in the living room and an electric wall fire in the front room. We only had enough money to buy a bedroom suite, a cot and chest of drawers for Carol's room and a carpet for the front room, and some rugs for the living room and bedroom. I had a small gas copper to boil whites, but no washing machine, dryer, refrigerator, vacuum cleaner or television. There was a 'pantry' which had a small window to allow it to stay cold, where we kept food. It was essential to shop most days.

Although the house had 'garage space', we did not have a car, so there was no need to dig out the space for a garage. If we had needed to it would have been a tremendous task, because the ground was solid chalk. Len spent the first Easter at this house trying to dig the solid chalk garden, ruining a couple of forks in the attempt. We put masses of top soil on so that we might grow some vegetables and flowers and grass. We found that cabbages loved the soil, but not much else. We had a lovely crop of thistles that were very happy with the chalk garden!

Carol was a good baby who slept through the night, even though she didn't like to sleep much during the day. Babies were put outside in their prams as soon as they had been fed in the morning to 'take the air'. The only times we did not put out the baby was when it was foggy or absolutely pouring with rain. It was a miracle that these babies survived such cold weather.

We attended Westbourne Street Church on Sunday mornings and one of us in the evening and Len also went in the afternoons to help with the Sunday school, mostly we walked with the pram. Len was an avid cricket fan and player and played for Westbourne Street cricket team with some of his brothers. So every Saturday during the summer he was off to various villages for a cricket match. I used to spend Saturday mornings praying for rain to come before 12 noon so that the match would be cancelled! I hated being left on Saturdays as well as the rest of the week. Sometimes I could go to watch, but with a baby it wasn't always convenient.

Len studied at 6.00am every morning, before his breakfast for his Accountancy exams while Carol was a baby and eventually became qualified. This was so that he could earn a little more money. I was not expected to go to work, there were no places to leave babies in those days, and Norah and William were far too old to help. Carol was a very bright, happy baby, who managed to stand up at eight months of age and walk by the time she was eleven months old. She was so inquisitive we could not leave anything open, because she would get into it if there was a space. She was always climbing things and one day was found half way up the window cleaner's ladder! She often fell off things and even downstairs a couple of times. There weren't any stair-gates in those days.

Because High Wycombe had an American Weather Station situated on the outskirts of the town, there were inevitably American Servicemen (airmen) around. When we put an advertisement in the local paper for a lodger—which we felt might help us to earn some money—we had a reply from a Major Gamage. Major Gamage was a pilot in the American air force and based at the weather station at High Wycombe. He was looking for a room, but no food. He also wanted someone to do his laundry. Both his requests were perfect for us, so we accepted him and he accepted us!

Immediately we went to town and bought a bedroom suite from our local store. We arranged to pay off the instalments on this bedroom suite over the next year or so, on a monthly basis. So when Major Gamage gave us his rent each month, we went into town and paid the amount off our full account, until eventually we owned the suite. Major Gamage was related to the 'Gamages' of the big store in London. He even owned some orange ranches in California. Every time he flew to a foreign country he brought back chocolates for us. Doing his laundry was easy for me, although it took a few weeks to turn out a shirt with a collar as stiff as a board. Every time he received the clean washing back he asked if I would use a little more starch, this I did until the collars were so stiff they felt like very strong card! Eventually I reached the required amount of stiffness! We were very sad when he was posted to Greece and had to leave us. I can honestly say he was never any trouble at all and he put up with any noise that we made when he was trying to sleep in the day time.

Len, Julie and I, joined by a friend called Pete, began to sing together in a quartet. We were invited to sing at functions in and around the Buckinghamshire area. Mostly we sang madrigals and entered a few competitions, doing very well. We named ourselves the Markham Singers. We once sang at a fete at a little village nearby called Finest where Tony Hancock was the guest who opened the fete.

Len and Pete also belonged to a male voice choir called Wycombe Orpheus Male Voice Choir and at least once a year it joined up with our Ladies Choir to sing in Wycombe Town Hall. These were exciting events, conducted by a few famous musicians, one of which was Muir Matheson who conducted music for films.

Every Friday Carol and I would go to Nora and William's house where Nora cooked us lunch. In the afternoon I would take Nora shopping in William's car. Len used to call in after work and have his tea with us all. We then would take a very tired and spoilt Carol home. One Friday Nora asked me not to bring Carol but to pick her up because she wanted to visit someone in hospital. We drove to the hospital concerned and on the way she asked to stop at a local shop where she asked me to go and buy a box of chocolates for the patient. When I returned with the box of chocolates, she told me they were for Hilda; because that was the person we were visiting. My mind went all over the place, why did I have to do this? I thought. When we arrived at the hospital we were ushered to the right ward and there in bed was Hilda recovering from a hysterectomy. I stood at the bedside, and awkwardly handed her the chocolates. She said "Thank you for visiting me and also for the chocolates". Nora continued to speak to her, but I again was speechless. My mind was in turmoil; wasn't I supposed to love this woman? What was wrong with me?

CHAPTER 15

*I*n spite of my vow to not have another baby, on 24th July 1956 Helen Julie, our second daughter was born at the Maternity Home in High Wycombe. She weighed 9lbs and was an adorable baby. I had a difficult time due to the fact that she was "face to pubes" and I suffered a post-partum haemorrhage at the birth which necessitated four pints of blood to be transfused. Unfortunately I had a bad reaction to the blood which had to be stopped before I had received the full amount. When I returned home I found it difficult to manage, as I was quite unwell. Len's Auntie May arrived to help us; she was certainly a God-send.

Life became very busy with two very small children. They were very well behaved little girls and we found we could take them anywhere and they seemed to know how to behave. When Helen was nine months old we returned to stay with Marjorie and her family in Bournemouth for a two week holiday. We hired a car for the journey and it was lovely to see Marjorie and her family again and we took her mother and father out a few times to various places around Bournemouth while we were there; they enjoyed that very much. We went everywhere on the bus using a pushchair that Len's sister Jackie had lent us. It was big enough to put both the girls into, plus all the bags. We found we walked miles pushing the girls, they were very well behaved and enjoyed playing on the sand and paddling in the sea.

Norah was becoming less and less active. She had only to walk a short distance before she was totally breathless. Her blood pressure was difficult to control. During this time I tried to take her out every week if she was well enough, and she thoroughly enjoyed having the children around her. She spoiled Carol so much, that she would be very naughty when we were at their house, but at home Carol was as good as gold. If Carol wanted anything that she saw in the shop window, Nora would rush inside and buy it for her, also buying a smaller edition for Helen. I continued to spend the whole day every Friday with Nora. She would cook some lunch for us and then we would all have a nap, then she might go with us on the bus to Wycombe to look around the shops if she was well enough. Both the girls enjoyed spending time with her. She used to keep some small bars of chocolate in her drawer by her chair, and both the girls knew that she would be giving them one each.

One morning William woke me up early and told me that Nora, aged 68, had died during the night. This was a great shock as we had been with her the day before and had spent a very happy day together. Nora seemed very happy that day. I really had no idea that it was her last day. I went back to William's house to see her and found her looking as if she were just asleep in her bed. I am sure she went to sleep and left this world whilst she was asleep. William was torn to pieces, he cried all the time and it was then left to me to make some of the arrangements. The minister from Westbourne Street Methodist Church came and arranged for the funeral to be there. William was so distressed he didn't particularly want any hymns for the service, but I told him he must have at least three! How young and inexperienced I was. When the day of the funeral came I was amazed to find I could not sing a note without crying; that taught me a lesson. Life seemed very strange without Nora. This was the point at which I began to think about Hilda. I suppose I missed my adopted mother so much that I needed a replacement; at this time I was 23 years old.

CHAPTER 16

$\mathcal{W}$e bought our first car, a second hand Ford Anglia. I was the only one able to drive, so we needed to get Len some driving lessons. This meant we could be much more mobile and the children wouldn't need to be wrapped up so much in warm clothing. Some days in the winter there were so many layers to put on the children we had to start well before we needed to go out, to enable us to be ready in time.

In 1960 Len was asked by his firm to move to the Cheltenham area to work as Financial Accountant of a new factory which they were opening at a place called Toddington, Gloucestershire. It was hard to tell William that we were about to leave him on his own. We chose a three bed roomed semi-detached house with a garage in a small village called Woodmancote at the foot of Cleeve Hill near Cheltenham racecourse. The area was very beautiful. Carol was ready to start school at this time and was given a place nearby; the school was at Bishops Cleeve. She started school accompanied by her cousin Donna, daughter of Len's Sister Daphne. Daphne and her husband Alf and their son Craig and daughter Donna had also moved to the area from High Wycombe with the same firm. Alf was to be Works Manager at Toddington factory. For a while they lived with us in our house until their new house was ready. Although there were three bedrooms, it was a bit of a squash for everyone. The four children slept in one room which was quite large and thoroughly enjoyed themselves.

We transferred our membership of the Methodist Church to Bishops Cleeve Methodist Church. It was a new modern small church built on a housing estate also near to Cheltenham Racecourse. The children enjoyed Sunday School and Len began to teach in the Sunday School as well. I found life at Woodmancote very lonely. I missed all my friends and the choir and singing. Although the house in which we lived was enjoyable, I think because it was at the end of a cul-de-sac, I saw very few people during the day when Len had gone to work, and the children to school. It might have been better if I could have worked for a few hours a day, but in those days there were no part time jobs to be had, especially for mothers with small children.

William came to stay with us many times while we lived at this new house. He loved gardening and spent his time in the garden replanting things that I had already planted! His excuse was that I had planted things upside down! He seemed very lonely without Nora and we both missed her very much.

CHAPTER 17

*T*hings began to look better and then I found out I was pregnant again. We all looked forward to the birth of our next child with excitement. I decided to have the baby at home and had no opposition to this idea from the local doctor, even though my past obstetric history was not good. I got to know the two midwives who lived nearby, one of which would be looking after me, depending who was on duty.

About a week before the birth I found I was leaking water and was told by the local GP "Don't make a fuss this is nothing to worry about and carry on as usual until the baby arrives". Later in my life I was to find out that this was not good advice at all and that I should have been admitted to a hospital as I might have developed an infection in the area around the baby or even suffered a prolapsed cord, which would have cut off the oxygen and food supply to the baby.

I woke up at 5.00am on Wednesday morning, 22nd March, and said to Len, "I think you had better ring for the midwife because I have lost some more water and this water has turned into a strange colour, and I am getting some pains". Len had to walk to the end of the road because we did not have a telephone in the house. One of the midwives duly arrived and examined me and said that she thought the baby would not arrive before late afternoon as the head was not engaged. After she had left I felt the pains coming very quickly and strongly and I urged Len to get the midwife back again. He went to the end of the road and telephoned again and was told that the midwife would get the student midwife to come and sit with me. She obviously did not think it was time for me to deliver. Unfortunately babies don't wait until the time is right!

Once Len had encouraged me to go upstairs to bed and I had told him he must "Get the midwife, now", he went to the house as the bottom of the garden where a friend lived rather than walk to the end of the road to telephone the midwife again. During this time I could not hold on any longer and the baby was born. She was very blue in colour and didn't seem to be breathing. Just at that moment my friend (from the bottom of the garden) arrived to sit with me! She tried to clear the baby's mouth and thought that the baby might be dead. All at once the midwife arrived in a great huff and puff. She was totally shocked to see that the baby had arrived and spent a few minutes working on her. Eventually the baby gave a cry which was more like a kitten mewing.

We called this new baby Ruth Gillian and she weighed 7lbs. When Len and I held her and studied her, after the midwives had gone, I said "She looks like Auntie Flo!" How strange that I should think of her; I wondered about Hilda again. I needed a mother at that moment. Over the next few weeks Ruth was very quiet and only cried like a kitten when she was desperately hungry. No one said anything about the birth or whether Ruth was OK, we just got on with the task of looking after our little family.

Just after Ruth was born, Norman rang me to tell me that William was dying with liver cancer. This was a great shock and we spent the next few weeks going back and forth to High Wycombe with our little family in tow to see him and encourage him to eat. Eventually he moved in with Connie and Norman and when Ruth was six weeks old he died. Now we had to arrange another funeral—I left the arrangements with Norman, I was not going to make the same mistake twice. The saddest part was clearing William's house out. All my childhood memories were to be wiped out in one afternoon! Norman had a big bonfire in William's garden, amongst all those lovely flowers that William grew. Many treasures were burnt on that bonfire; Norman was quite ruthless and didn't want to keep anything. It was his father and I was only adopted. At this time I felt very lonely and rejected. I was 27 years old.

CHAPTER 18

*T*he time after this death and Ruth's rapid arrival into the world left me below par in my health. I spent a few weeks with boils and sinus trouble, until eventually I began to feel better.

I missed my singing and I felt very lonely in this beautiful village. I didn't feel part of the church, because I was always busy with my small children. Len was busy with his work and was often late home. All in all, I desperately wanted my mother! Any mother!

We suddenly received news that Len's father was ill in hospital, so off we went again, travelling backwards and forwards to High Wycombe. Len's father died in hospital when Ruth was fourteen months old. Both Len and I felt devastated by yet another parental loss, so soon after the others.

Five years after we had arrived in Cheltenham we got another call from Len's managers that they required him back at High Wycombe. So off we went again, moving back to our roots. We bought a three bed roomed detached house on Green Hill, which overlooked the Hughenden valley. I had a wonderful view from my kitchen window. Because the house was on the top of a hill, it looked across the valley to the next hill, which happened to be Hughenden Park, the home of Disraeli.

We settled in very well and had some lovely neighbours. Carol and Helen attended my old Junior School. It had changed a lot since I was there in the '40s. It had some decent toilets now and the food was better! Carol was 10 and Helen was 9 and Ruth attended the local playgroup in Hazlemere. I used to take Ruth to the playgroup on the back of my bike. She says even today she remembers being on the back of my bike and stopping after nursery to buy some cakes in the bakers shop.

When Carol was about 10 years old we had the awful news that my brother Norman had died suddenly of a heart attack. Carol wept a great deal and felt that she would not be able to see her Auntie Connie again; she had to be reassured that Connie was still alive. Norman was just 47 years old and at this point I was 29 years old. We all felt devastated at the loss of Norman and I knew I would miss his brotherly advice.

One day Carol fell in the garden and caught her mouth on the clothes line which unfortunately pulled out her front permanent tooth. The children who were playing with her in the garden searched on the lawn and found her tooth. We tried to put it back in but Carol was too upset for us to persevere. I felt this was a great disaster, because her future life without her tooth flashed before my eyes. Len, on the other hand thought it was nothing to get too excited about. Her future without that tooth has caused so many problems I really feel for her.

CHAPTER 19

*W*e realised that Ruth had 'Learning Difficulties' and needed help at school. She was a clumsy child, always falling—part of the effect of brain damage, caused by a lack of oxygen at birth. She fell down the front steps of the house at Green Hill and fractured her skull and ended up in Hospital for a few days, until she was pronounced well enough to come home. It was quite a worry managing to keep her from falling and hurting herself again. She was a very frustrated child and would lash out at the others when things didn't go right. Because Helen was always trying to help Ruth, it was Helen who very often got bitten by Ruth. She attended various doctors, clinics and educational psychologists, who all agreed she had brain damage which was scattered throughout her brain, affecting so many abilities.

We joined Wesley Methodist Church in High Wycombe and the children settled into the Sunday School. We had not been in the house very long before I was pronounced pregnant again—goodness me, how many more times? Louise Kathryn was born at The Maternity Home, High Wycombe on 30th December 1964 at 8pm weighing in at 7lbs 10oz. I went home after two days, very different from my first two babies. Len's mother, Louisa, came to stay for a few days to help out and this made things much easier for us both. Louise was a lovely baby, but she did not want to sleep at all. The older girls tell me now that they can remember her crying when they wanted to sleep. She loved to cat-nap, but not to sleep for any length of time. The crying eventually ended up as singing and undressing as she grew older! I think she was practising to be a singing strip-tease artist! If she had been the first baby things would have been OK, but when there were three others all trying to sleep, it didn't make for a very peaceful time. At night we had to leave a radio playing outside her bedroom to help induce sleep.

I re-joined the Chiltern Ladies Choir and sang with Julie and some other friends of mine. We started singing duets again at local churches around the area and Len also re-joined the High Wycombe Male Voice Choir. A small contingent of the Chiltern Ladies Choir was called on from time to time to sing at the crematorium (when the mourners requested) at funerals. We were paid the princely sum of £1 each for a funeral. So you could say I became a professional singer at last!

One of the ladies in the choir had a general stores shop which was within walking distance of our house, and she asked me if I would work in the shop three evenings a week. I thoroughly enjoyed this, especially as I had never done anything like it before. I loved meeting all the people who came in the shop. I also answered an advert from the Bible Lands Society which was situated quite near our home. They took me on to be an outworker, packing Christmas cards and Christmas gifts. All the family worked on this job in the evenings and my neighbours joined in during afternoons. Everyone was sharing my wages! It was good fun and we all had great conversations while we were occupied!

When we had lived in this house for approximately 5 years Len was instructed by his company to go to live in the Manchester area and supervise as Financial Director a new factory at Whitefield. You can imagine our shock, because we had settled in this house very well and never ever thought about moving again. Carol was settled in her new school at Hazlemere and Helen had just been informed that she had passed the 11+ exam and would get a place at Wycome Girls Grammar School in September.

Len and I and Louise, who was two and a half, journeyed to Whitefield on the train and then a hired a car to seek out a new residence for our little family. I had never been north of Birmingham and thought that Manchester would be a terrible place for all of us. How wrong I was. We viewed many houses around the area but eventually chose one in Bury, which is very close to Whitefield where the factory was. This was a four bed roomed, detached house with a large flat garden. How lovely it would be to garden a flat garden, the two gardens we had already had at High Wycombe were so hilly that gardening was a hard chore. We felt this one would be easy. The children could even have a swing in the garden. As we would not be able to move until November, there was a problem for Helen who needed to start a new school in Bury in September. Luckily for us a neighbour of ours at Wycombe had moved from Bury a few years earlier and knew a lady who was living in Bury and would give Helen a bed until we moved into the area. As you can imagine this did not go down well with Helen, but we had no choice, because if we let her start her new school in Wycombe we would then have to start her again at another school after about eight weeks. Both schools insisted that we provided the full uniform which would have been very costly. Helen was eventually taken by Len to Bury and left at the house of Mr and Mrs Andrews. Len said they were lovely people and she would be OK with them. He managed to accompany her to the school on her first day which he hoped would make it easier for her. Helen still tells us how much she hated being there, but I am sure Mr and Mrs Andrews did their very best and we too felt it was the best way to deal with a big problem.

CHAPTER 20

*W*e moved to Bury on the 4th November 1968. The day of moving was very wet, in fact pouring with rain, and when we arrived at the house the first thing we saw was our beloved new piano standing on the drive with rain splashing all over it. The removal van had arrived too soon for us. The neighbours were very friendly and helped with a cup of tea. I left the four children in the lounge with the gas fire lit to keep them warm while I went to the local shop and purchased some cakes and bread for their lunch. The central heating was provided by a solid fuel boiler in the kitchen, and getting this to light was a nightmare. Later in the day when we had finished moving things around there was a knock at the door and the Minister of Bury Central Methodist Church stood on the doorstep. He said his wife would give us a cooked tea if we would like to call on her, although he would not be there because he was off to a meeting; you can imagine how she might have felt if we had turned up on her doorstep asking for a cooked tea for six of us! Needless to say, we went off in search of a restaurant that was open in the evening for a cooked meal. The next day was "Bonfire Night" and the neighbours invited us to a large bonfire in the adjoining field; very useful for us because we had plenty of packaging to get rid of, and

I am sure the neighbours were pleased that we brought more bonfire materials, perhaps that was why they invited us!.

On the first Sunday we were at our new house we ventured into Bury in the thick fog of the day and found Bury Central Methodist Church. Len and I were not happy with this church due to a lack of children in the Sunday School. On the day we attended, our children doubled the total count of children! We eventually found another church Whitefield Methodist, nearer to home, but actually in Whitefield, and were warmly welcomed by the church family. The Sunday School was large, so there were plenty of children for ours to get friendly with.

We settled very well and Carol, Helen ad Ruth got on well at their local schools. A year after starting at her school Carol was transferred to the same school as Helen because she passed the 13+ exam. Len's mum came to stay with us on a few occasions and was very helpful in the garden, her speciality was collecting slugs!

Ruth was acting very oddly at times, she started jerking and then she would do something odd, like one night when she ran out of the house in the pouring rain with only her nightdress on. Len ran along the road in his socks to catch her; they both got very wet! After these sporadic events Ruth used to sleep for hours.

Ruth was now diagnosed properly with brain damage due to anoxia (lack of oxygen) probably at birth. She was assessed and given an IQ of around 68 which was fairly low. She was described as having 'Learning Difficulties'. She was also diagnosed as having epilepsy. She was given medication to prevent her having fits. Various people gave us snippets of information on how to deal with all this, but nothing was very helpful. We attended various clinics again, but they were not much help.

CHAPTER 21

*L*en and I applied to join the Halle Chorus in Manchester. We went for an audition, and both passed. I sang in the second soprano section and Len sang in the first bass section. Sir John Barbirolli was the resident conductor of the Halle at the time and we were able to visit many places where we sang with him conducting. Whilst we were in the choir we met a couple who originated in High Wycome. Margaret and Trevor were about Len's age and knew some of the same people that Len knew in his younger days at High Wycombe. We had many joyful family 'get togethers' with them, especially at Christmas times. Trevor played flute and Margaret played the piano, our children and theirs were all learning instruments so we all joined together and sang and played Christmas Carols around the piano as well as playing many games together.

Cath, my friend across the road and I joined the band of volunteers to deliver 'Meals on Wheels'. We met some very interesting characters! One of our calls was shocking, we found the customer lying dead on the floor. One day while delivering the meals I found my left breast was extremely swollen and sore, so I went to the doctors who sent me to the casualty department at the local hospital. The consultant said I had a lump in the breast and needed to be admitted and have the lump removed. This was a trying time for Len and me, as we were both concerned that it might be cancer. I went into hospital and had the operation and found that the surgeon had removed half of the breast, because he said the lump was enormous. I stayed in hospital for a few days before eventually returning home. The lump turned out to be a fibro adenoma, which was not a cancer. A year later I had to have another lump removed from the right breast which was also a fibro adenoma.

Soon after this visit to hospital, I became depressed. I felt worthless and not of any use. I suppose it was the stress of hospital, operation and anxiety about the outcomes and then the fact that the children didn't need me as much. Some people would call it Post Traumatic Stress Syndrome. I very rarely saw much of Len; he was at work from early until late and then he brought work home with him. I longed for more conversation with people. After a few weeks I began to feel better and thought about what I could do for the future to prevent it happening again. I reached a stage where I needed to get out and use my brain.

I enrolled for O level English at the local college and was successful in obtaining a pass at level 1. So I was not as rusty as I thought! I enrolled for Human Biology and passed at level 2. Having met another similar family as ourselves on the estate, Cath and I enrolled for Geography A level and English Literature A level. We both passed the English but both failed the Geography. Well you can't win everything!

I decided that I wanted to be a nurse, but Len was adamant that it would not fit in with the family, so I said I would apply for Teacher Training instead and he agreed that would be best for the family. I managed to get a place at a mature teachers' college in Manchester. When I had completed one week at this college I realised that I was pregnant again; what awful timing this was. I rang the principal and told him I needed to defer my training until the following year—ever an optimist, me! Within a couple of weeks I suffered a miscarriage; how devastating.

Now what was I to do? "I <u>will</u> be a nurse. I know that is what I should do", I told Len "I have always wanted to be a nurse". He was still adamant that it would not fit in with the family. I knew that he was right, but something drove me on. I telephoned Hope Hospital and asked if they would have me to train as a midwife on a direct entry course that they had. I went for an interview and was accepted to commence my midwifery training on the 1st January 1971.

Life at home completely changed for all of us except Len. We all made sure Len didn't notice anything different about his life! Carol and Helen were excellent at looking after Ruth and Louise. Although I have no idea how they behaved with each other when I was not present! We worked out rotas and special duties to share between us and Carol and Helen excelled themselves. I tried hard to swap my duties around so that I could get as many split shifts as possible. This meant starting at 7.30am and coming home at 1.00pm, so that I could do washing, ironing, shopping and cooking. I then left at 4.30pm once the children were in for tea and completed my day's work, finishing at 10.00pm. How I found enough energy to complete two years of this I will never know, but being determined helped a great deal. I enjoyed learning all about nursing and midwifery. The worst problem I had was that some of the sisters on the various wards were absolute tartars! They certainly made one's life difficult.

CHAPTER 22

*R*uth was assessed again, due to her Learning Difficulties and we were advised that she should go to a special boarding school in Lostock. The school was entitled "School for the Delicate". There were many children there who were not delicate in the true sense of the word, but social misfits. This was disastrous, because Ruth learnt many unsocial attributes, such as spitting across the dinner table and swearing at everyone. Ruth was taken by Len on a Sunday afternoon and picked up by Len or myself on a Friday night, depending on who was available. Once when Len was supposed to pick her up he was involved in a car accident, but luckily was not badly injured. One Friday I picked up Ruth from school and found she was covered in bruises and some of her hair had been pulled out due to some of the girls beating her up. When we reached home I rang the headmaster and told him I would not be sending her to that school again if that was what was to happen to her. She was sent back to the local Primary School, where she settled in well. She did need remedial help with all subjects.

I passed the first part of the midwifery exam after 18 months training, and then transferred to Fairfield General Hospital in Bury to complete the part 2. The first three months of this part of the course was to be spent working in hospital and the second part working on the district.

We went on holiday to Wales when I had completed part 1 of the course, and when we came home Helen had contracted infective hepatitis. She was very poorly for a few weeks. As I was not allowed to work with mothers and babies because of the possibility of me acquiring the same infection, I had to stay off work for a while. This necessitated adding a few extra weeks to my course. During this time Len had a mild heart attack and was advised to rest at home for a while. This was a worrying time for all of us, but Helen and I kept Len company as we were both at home. In fact it gave me time to do some decorating with Len advising from his chair!

My midwife mentor on the district was a lovely lady called Sister White who lived just around the corner from our house. She was lovely to work with and I learned a great deal from her about people. She would visit anyone who was in need in her spare time. People whom she helped said she was like an angel.

I delivered my first baby in someone's home with no supervision at all. At last I had reached the standard I desired to be. I decided that I was going to be the very best midwife that I could. While I was in this part of the training I unfortunately suffered a ruptured ovarian cyst which necessitated having an operation. This added another three months to my training due to the time I was off sick. I felt I was never going to complete the course and become a qualified midwife.

The time came for the exam at the end of the training and I was overjoyed to know that I passed. I was given a full time job at Fairfield General Hospital as a staff nurse/midwife. It was hard work, but I enjoyed every moment of it.

When my next weeks off came round we decided to go on holiday abroad, for the first time, to Minorca, which obviously necessitated an aeroplane flight. I was so nervous—but I found the experience superb. So Len and I and Ruth and Louse enjoyed our stay in the lovely sunshine.

CHAPTER 23

*S*uddenly I was pregnant again. Len and I were devastated. The doctor offered me a termination and Len thought that perhaps I should obey him, but I could not kill my unborn baby just because he/she did not fit into our timetable. I carried on working until one day at about six months pregnant I went into early labour. This meant a long stay in hospital. Carol had already gone to teacher training college in Liverpool, so all the caring for Ruth and Louise was on Helen's shoulders. She was busy preparing for her A levels, so it was a very stressful time. Helen came to visit me in the afternoons and sat and cried about the things she had to cope with, especially looking after Ruth who was difficult. I had many guilty pangs about not being at home doing the job of mother. Eventually I was allowed out of hospital and I was told I could not work until after the baby was born. I resigned my job and took out my Superannuation money which helpfully bought a pram and cot, etc. because I expected to be at home for a while with this new baby not working.

Life went on and I became bigger and bigger! My ankles swelled and my blood pressure began to rise. I sailed past the due date which was not surprising because all my other children had been two weeks late according to dates. On Good

Friday 1974, I was advised to go into hospital to be induced, as my blood pressure was really too high. Reluctant as I was, I also realised that this might get rid of the huge bump I was carrying around and I did really feel tired and weary. When I arrived in hospital, the doctor tried to break my waters, but he said the head was too high, so he put me on a drip to start the labour. Within a couple of hours I was getting regular strong contractions and was transferred to the delivery room because the sister on duty thought I might be rushing along and would soon deliver! I laboured on for the rest of Friday, all day Saturday and up to 8.00pm on Sunday; my word was I tired. The doctor decided to use forceps because the baby was not in a satisfactory position and I was getting very tired, but the sister in charge who was very experienced suggested that she herself should turn the head, as she thought the baby was in deep transverse position, therefore never going to be born naturally in that position. She did indeed turn his head and by 10.15 p.m Charles Jason Michael was born, weighing 9lbs 8ozs. I was so tired I was completely disinterested, but Len, who came in after he was born, was highly delighted to have a son. By the next day I too was interested and amazed at having a son after all those daughters. The children were ecstatic and wanted to pick him up and kiss him all the time. He was a very contented baby who had so much love that he surely would be the happiest adult alive when he grew up.

By the time Charles was 6 weeks old he was baptised at Whitefield Methodist Church and we had a party for our friends. One of my midwife friends who came to the party suggested I could do one night a week as a midwife at a hospital in Accrington where apparently there was a vacancy. After talking to Len he agreed and I applied, only to be told that I was needed more at Bull Hill Maternity Home, Darwen, for three days a week! Helen had finished her A levels and was keen to look after Charles, instead of finding a temporary job for the summer. So off I went for two weekdays and one weekend day (when Len was at home) and I became a midwife again. Helen shared my salary instead of her trying to find a short time job nearby. I thoroughly enjoyed Bull Hill and the people I worked with, but by the winter the travelling over the moors late at night and early mornings was awful, very foggy and wet. I decided to apply in Bury for a job instead and was given one at Bealey Maternity Home, Radcliffe, just five minutes from my house. The terms were the same as Darwen and I settled in very well. When Helen went off to Addenbrooks Hospital in Cambridge to train as a nurse, I made arrangements with my friend Cath to have Charles for two days a week and Len to have him at one weekend day. Cath became a registered child-minder and I paid her the going rate, although she was reluctant to have the money. Cath also had four daughters of similar ages as our own. So he went from one house of women to another. He had a good life and lots of love from all these doting women! I loved spending time with Charles on my days off. He and I spent many happy hours together.

CHAPTER 24

$\mathcal{C}$arol met Mark at college and they eventually married at Whitefield Methodist Church in 1976. They had both trained as teachers and managed to get jobs in Liverpool, so they rented a flat in Liverpool. It was a lovely wedding which was celebrated at Bury Elizabethan Suite with all their friends and of course both families. Helen, Ruth and Louise were bridesmaids and Charles as pageboy (when we could get him to stand still) and they all looked lovely.

We went on holiday again, but this time Carol and Mark, Helen, Louise, Ruth, Charles and my friend Julie who was by then separated from her husband and feeling lonely. We went to Majorca and had a lovely time together.

When Charles was four years old, I needed to have a hysterectomy due to fibroids and this was performed at Fairfield General Hospital; I recovered well. At the time Helen was at home recuperating from her first hip operation, so I was very well cared for by her, as she was by me. Helen had problems with pain in her hip and had an operation to clean up the hip joint which had dislocated. This was very painful for her.

Charles eventually started school at Sunny Bank School and it was about this time that the Maternity Home I was working in was going to be closed down and made into a community hospital. I applied for a Community Midwife post and was successful, but had to work full time. This fitted in very well, because Charles was now settled in School and Cath was always at home when school finished. Again it was hard work but rewarding.

I thoroughly enjoyed being a Community Midwife. It meant I could arrange my work as I pleased, except when I was called to a delivery. I had many deliveries, some during the day but many during the night. I always found that home deliveries were a wonderful experience for the patient, but also for me. Everyone in the house seemed much more relaxed than when in a hospital. Less pain killers were used for the mother, due to her ability to relax.

In 1978 Helen married Derek; they were both nurses working at Addenbrooks hospital in Cambridge. The wedding was celebrated at Radcliffe Civic Hall. Louise and Ruth were bridesmaids and Charles page boy. It was a lovely wedding with loads of people present. Helen and Derek went to live in a Mobile Home in Cambridge, not far from the hospital.

While Helen was working at Addenbrooks, she had more trouble with her hip. The doctors weren't sure what was wrong but she ended up with two more operations. During this time she had to have an abortion because she had an x-ray before they realised she was pregnant. This was extremely upsetting for them as it was for all of us. Eventually, as she became pregnant again, she saw, privately, a consultant at Manchester who said she needed a hip replacement, but not until she had had her baby. Helen and Derek then moved to Radcliffe so that they could be near me to enable me to look after the baby while she had her operation. Derek decided to be a policeman and went for his training. Karen was born in 1981, a beautiful baby—it made me cry when I saw her in the nursery at the hospital, I just wanted to cuddle her all day. Fancy me being a grandmother; I wondered what my two mums would think.

Helen had her first hip replacement when Karen was 15 months old. Karen moved in with us for six weeks to enable Helen to get better quickly. When Karen was 9 years old George was born. Now we had two grandchildren, how wonderful.

Ruth was now working at Victoria Station in Manchester as a canteen assistant. She used to push the trolley around the café collecting dirty pots and cleaning the tables. The manageress was really good to Ruth. If she found Ruth was being stroppy she used to send her to another room until Ruth calmed down. That way she could do her job fairly well with good supervision.

Len and I, Carol and Mark, Louise and her boy-friend, Curt, my friend Julie and Charles went to Torremolinos in Spain and thoroughly enjoyed our holiday together in the sun. While we were there Charles fell off a horse and had to spend a couple of days in a Spanish hospital with concussion. He recovered well and enjoyed the rest of the holiday.

CHAPTER 25

*W*hen Louise was 18 years old she gained a place at Birmingham School of Music to study violin and piano. We were all thrilled with this. Unfortunately she had only been there for six weeks when she came home for a weekend. She told me she had back pain, so I sent her to the doctors who then in turn sent her to a gynaecologist. The gynaecologist said she had a large mass in the abdomen and she wasn't sure whether it was on the ovary or in the uterus. Louise went into hospital and had a large ovarian tumour removed. Later that week the gynaecologist called at the house to tell us that the tumour was cancer. The cancer was a dysgermanoma which was quite rare and only found in young girls. It would necessitate radiotherapy for Louise at Christie Hospital, the nearest cancer specialist hospital.

We then embarked on five and a half weeks of radiotherapy which made Louise very sick and unwell. She was an excellent patient, never grumbling and always listening to advice. It was so sad to see her so unwell. For the first week of treatment she stayed in the hospital, but she was very unhappy and lost a lot of weight due to the fact that meals were only served at certain times, and those times she was being sick so could not eat. I managed to persuade the consultant that she would be better at home and that is what happened. All our friends and church members were very willing to take her to Christie's if I was working, so she completed the five and half weeks, looking less and less well as time went on. Following the treatment, she began to pick up and she started a diet of uncooked vegetables and vitamins called "The Bristol Diet". The church family was praying for her all the time and so were many other people around the country. Even the local Roman Catholic Priest came to see her and gave her a blessing.

Louise had a friend from school that lived quite close to us who used to call in after school to see and sit with Louise. She turned out to be a real angel, sitting doing her homework while Louise was snoozing; and making me a cup of tea when I returned home from work exhausted. Many times I would drop off to sleep before drinking the tea and when awake finding that she had gone home. Poor girl she must have thought us both very odd, always sleeping, but anxiety and radiology takes its toll!

As soon as she felt better, Louise returned to Birmingham once a week for violin lessons so that she would keep up her standard of playing for the future. She returned to Birmingham full time in the following September, only to find, after a few weeks, a new lump appear in her neck. A telephone call to Christie hospital and one blast of radiation treatment and back she went to continue with her studies.

While Louise was convalescing, Ruth failed to return home one evening after work. We were out of our minds with worry. We eventually found her living with an old man in a house off Cheetham Hill Road, Manchester! She had decided that she would marry this man, who was called John. Nothing we said or did would persuade her not to marry him; in fact she phoned one Saturday to tell us she had just got married! She moved into to a high rise flat with him in Miles Platting.

It was a tremendous worry to Len and me and indeed to all the family. We tried to keep in contact as much as we could, but it was very difficult because he (John) was very hostile to us.

I had a telephone call one day from a man who said he was John's son and that I should get Ruth out of his house and back home, because "My dad is a Crook; he is teaching Ruth to go out shoplifting" he said. I felt even worse about the situation, but found there was not much I could do if Ruth didn't want to come home and of course they were married, so I had no rights.

CHAPTER 26

One day I came home from work at lunch time and received a phone call from Cath (my friend) who said that Ruth had arrived at her house. I hurried over there, and sure enough Ruth was sitting on Cath's sofa 'as bold as brass'. What a surprise that was. She told us that she had run away from John because he had been locking her in the flat and also knocking her about. She only had with her the clothes she was wearing and a handbag, in which there was no money or anything else, for that matter. I called Derek and asked him "What shall I do?" He told me "Do not take her to your home, because if you do the social services will not help Ruth at all". This was a very hard decision to make, after all Ruth was my daughter and there was a room for her at my house.

After much telephoning we went to look at a room in a hostel in Longsight—this was not suitable so we went to a 'doss house' in Prestwich, which I declined as it was filthy and there were no locks on the doors and the house was full of men! At last a lady telephoned us and instructed us to go the Women's Refuge in Radcliffe. Len could not go as men were barred. There was a lovely room awaiting Ruth and her own cupboard in the kitchen for her food and also washing facilities, etc. Cath and I were happy to leave Ruth with a wonderful lady manageress who welcomed her and said she would deal with everything that Ruth needed.

When we saw Ruth after a couple of days, this lady had arranged a court order barring John from seeing Ruth, arranged the start of proceedings for a divorce, registered her with a doctor and obtained all the benefits to which she was allotted by the government. How right Derek was, I would never have known how to start, yet this lady had done it all in two days! Ruth stayed at the refuge for about eight weeks until the lady managed to obtain a Council flat in Bury for her. Ruth moved into the flat and we helped her with some furniture, etc. A few years later she met and married Paul who was a few years younger than herself.

Len and I, Carol and Mark and Charles went on holiday to Yugoslavia. Although we enjoyed the holiday, Carol and Mark did not seem to be getting on with each other as well as before. Yugoslavia was a beautiful country but poor, probably due to being still under Communism. Nothing had been modernised.

Louise eventually obtained her degree in music and a diploma in conducting and decided that a fourth year at the University would help her to achieve success in her search for a job. Half way through the course she decided to get married to Curt (her boyfriend). Louise and Curt were eventually married at Whitefield Methodist Church on 28th August 1986. It was a lovely wedding with all our friends and family to help us to celebrate. The surgeon who operated on Louise when she was ill was present and took some photographs which were lovely. They bought a tiny house in Tottington and moved in as soon as they could. Louise became a peripatetic violin/piano teacher in Bury and Bolton. She also decided to do some modelling as well and modelled for the new Ford Mondeo of the time, actually travelling to Spain to carry out the modelling. She was also pictured on the back of the cornflake packet. Ruth was very keen to show everyone her picture and when she went shopping to the supermarkets she spent time turning all the packets round so that Louise's picture was at the front! Eventually Louise applied for and got a job as a medical representative with a Pharmaceutical Company. She was very happy to give up her peripatetic work and earn a better salary

Len and I went on a foreign holiday most years and one of those years was when Len was told he was redundant from the firm where he had worked for thirty three years. This was very hard for Len and while we were on holiday in Crete, we discussed how we would manage with a great deal less money. Len was lucky and got another job very quickly, although he never was paid as much salary again. Charles was upset that he would be as poor as another boy in his class and would not be able to have any more sweets. We reassured him that there would be enough money for him.

In 1986 Mark left Carol to live with someone else. As you can imagine, this caused her great distress, as it did the rest of us. Mark had always been a valued member of the family, everyone liked him and we also were going to miss him greatly. Carol and Mark had sold their house and were in the throes of buying another when this happened, so Carol did not have a house to live in. She went to live with a friend in Liverpool during the week, to enable her to work and came home to us at weekends. Eventually she bought a small house in Liverpool and moved in. She eventually met Jim and married him and sometime later their daughter Jane was born, our third grandchild.

CHAPTER 27

*L*en's health deteriorated, he suffered from angina and was not as able as before to cope with gardening, decorating and repairs. We decided to move to a bungalow nearby to where our large house was. The move went well and we settled into our 'last' place, we thought!

In 1991 Len complained of feeling very unwell and when he had seen the GP, he was sent to see a cardiac consultant who advised him to be admitted immediately to hospital, because he seemed to be having small heart attacks at the time. After having an angiogram which showed his cardiac arteries to be totally blocked and only one thin artery which had grown as an extra was left to feed the whole of the heart, he had a By-pass operation in which he had seven grafts attached in place of the diseased arteries. He recovered very well and was a good patient at home.

While this problem was unravelling, Helen donated some eggs to be fertilised by Curt for him and Louise to be able to have a baby of their own, because due the radiotherapy Louise's remaining ovary had been killed off, therefore no eggs. It was quite difficult driving from one hospital to another to visit first Len, then Helen. Luckily they were both patients in hospitals in Manchester.

Unfortunately Louise's marriage was also doomed—Curt left to live with another woman, leaving Louise totally distressed. Curt decided on his own, without telling Louise that he wanted the donor eggs destroyed, which by this time had been fertilised and frozen, awaiting their choice to have them by IVF treatment. This was the last straw for Louise; she went from being upset to angry and back again. Helen was also very upset that she had gone through all the trouble of donating eggs just for him to destroy them without any discussion with anyone. It nearly broke my heart to see them so distressed. Some years later Louise met Mike and eventually married him. Mike had three daughters of his own from his first marriage which had broken up, so now Louise had a ready-made little family to bring up.

In 1997 Helen and Derek decided to separate. They were not feeling able to live together. Derek bought a little house in Ramsbottom.

One day in 1998 the police called to see Julie to tell her that Derek had died. Helen, Karen and George were devastated, as the whole family were. It transpired that Derek had suffered a brain haemorrhage; he was only 42 years old.

The funeral took place at Whitefield Methodist Church led by the minister and was attended by loads of policemen. Travelling from Helen's house to the church we had a police escort on motorbikes who ushered us through the town and through the red traffic lights! Helen was very badly affected and took a long time to feel better. She told us that the week before Derek died, he had called to see her and they sat in the garden in the sun drinking coffee together. Derek then told her he loved her and could he come back now, but Helen said perhaps they should wait a while longer. She never saw him alive again.

In 1995 Len and I went to Australia; it was a cricket tour. We flew to Kuala Lumpur, where we changed planes, then on to Melbourne. We arrived on Christmas Eve. On Christmas Day the weather was so hot that we could hardly go out, but we had a lovely Christmas lunch together with the others on the tour. We missed being with our family, but managed to speak to them on the telephone. On Boxing Day the temperature had fallen drastically and it rained so that the cricket was cancelled for that day. We were able to attend the next day to watch the cricket.

After a few days we flew to Sydney and celebrated New Year by sailing round the harbour on a beautiful boat on which we had a lovely dinner and watched the fireworks. Sydney Harbour Bridge was lit up with fireworks for ages, it was spectacular. I heard later that the fireworks were a rehearsal for the next year which was the Millennium.

I was poorly with a chest infection while we were in Sydney, but we still had a good time and eventually flew back to Kuala Lumpur and then on to Penang, where we stayed for a few days before flying back to Kuala Lumpur and then on to Heathrow and eventually home. What a wonderful holiday that was to be able to visit the other side of the world!

Later we went to California on a tour where we met a couple called Jack and Muriel. During the tour we visited the Grand Canyon, Las Vegas, Bryce Canyon, San Francisco, Anaheim and San Diego. All the hotels we stayed in were comfortable and we visited so many places and learnt a great deal about the United States. We had a wonderful courier who explained the flora and fauna of that country and showed us videos of how the Indians were treated in the past.

The next year we went to Canada with Jack and Muriel on another tour and travelled from the Eastern side through the Rockies to Vancouver. We visited Quebec, Montreal, Toronto, the Niagara Falls, then flew across the country to the Rockies and then on to Vancouver, where we flew home to England again. The scenery of this country was amazing, making it a memorable tour.

CHAPTER 28

*I*n 1999 I kept getting a feeling that I needed to meet up again with Hilda, my birth mother. When I talked about this with Len he reminded me that by now she would be around ninety years old if she had lived, but was probably dead. But nothing could deter this feeling of need. I telephoned an 'Adoption' Company in Manchester and talked to a very kind lady who said she would help me. The first thing that I needed to do was to go to the Manchester Registry Office and look up the marriage of Hilda. For the next few weeks, when I had time, I went to study the records. The staff in the office got to know me quite well. I knew Hilda's married name was 'Hawkinson' and luckily there were very few people with that name and in no time at all I found her marriage. Also in these records I found my maternal grandmother's marriage details. I then looked up any children with that surname and soon found Valerie's birth details. I looked up Valerie's marriage and found she was now named Pratt. When I spoke to the very helpful lady from 'Adoption', she said she would look up the address of Valerie Pratt. She came back to me to tell me that there was no one of that name, but that a Valerie Hawkinson lived at Monks Risborough, Bucks. My next task was to write to Valerie. I sent a letter straight away enclosing a stamped addressed envelope and asked if she was the Valerie who used to stay at my house when we were girls? If she was not, would she please let me know, so that I would not bother her again? Within three days a reply came from Valerie, expressing her delight that I had now found my half-sister. She said she had always wanted to know where I was and to see me. In the letter she said "Mum sends her love"! This statement made me cry.

I showed the letter to Len who seemed to take forever to read it. He then turned to me and said "She doesn't use many full stops, does she?" How could he miss the point? How did he not understand how I was feeling.

I immediately rang Valerie and asked for Hilda's address and telephone number. I had to tell someone about the letter and rushed round to Helen's house, I knew she would understand how I was feeling. Helen was very helpful and sat me down with a cup of coffee and a chocolate biscuit (her cure for crying!). I felt a great deal of support from her and leant heavily on her for decisions on how I went forward from there. I felt I wanted to get in the car and race down to Waterlooville, near Portsmouth, where Hilda was now living, but Helen urged me to wait a day or to and to ring Hilda to suggest that I came down to see her. She said I needed to wait to see if Hilda wanted to see me. I rang Hilda and told her I wanted to see her. She said "Come tomorrow!" Did this mean she wanted me or not? What a torture this all was, I really had no idea how Hilda felt about me.

It was all arranged and a couple of days later Len and I flew to Southampton, hiring a car at Southampton airport and driving to Waterlooville. It was surprisingly easy to find the large building in which Hilda had her little flat. Hilda had remarried when her first husband died and her name was now Smith. Goodness me, if I had known that it would have taken years to find her! Mr Smith had died some years before.

When I spoke to Hilda on the phone she told me that the door would be on the latch, so to come straight in, she would be expecting me.

I arrived at her flat and asked Len to sit in the car while I went inside on my own, as this was something I had to face alone. I was very nervous, because I had no idea if she would welcome me or not as my treatment of her in the past was not very good. I had bought a pot plant to give to her as a gift; I chose this because I knew absolutely nothing of her likes and dislikes; a plant was so insignificant as to be OK.

The door was on the latch and when I knocked she shouted "Come in." My heart was racing very fast and suddenly I was standing in front of this elderly, white haired old lady who was sitting in a comfortable chair facing the door. We looked at each other and both said "Hello". Then, feeling very uncomfortable, as it didn't seem to be going well, I said "I have brought a plant for you, shall I put it on the window sill?" She answered "Yes". When I returned to face her, she suddenly said "You are the nurse, aren't you?" I replied "No, I'm your Jen". With that she hugged me close and cried tears all over me and I joined in with my tears.

What a moment, it made my heart turn over and beat extremely fast. How does she feel about me, I wondered, this person who chose another instead of her and pretty much ignored her in the past? We sat and talked for half an hour, when she suddenly said "Where is your husband, Len?" I told her he was waiting outside, so she urged me to bring him in. We spent the day reminiscing together. I wanted to ask many unanswered questions that were in my head, but it was difficult to keep this old lady on the subject. Later in the day two of my half-brothers, Andrew and James, arrived to meet me. They told me that she had told them about me only the day before we arrived, although Andrew said he seemed to know a bit about me, but James was amazed, he couldn't take his eyes off me, and I was the same with him. There seemed to be a very strong bond here. They both seemed very happy to meet me and both of them gave me a kiss and a hug. The brothers and sisters I had were Valerie, Andrew, Jill, James, Rupert and Evelyn. We took some photographs and then Len and I left in the hired car to drive to Southampton airport to fly home. What a wonderful day that was to have Hilda accept me as her daughter, after all those years of feeling neglected and rejected. How I wish I had found her before then. We had so much to learn about each other. I found it hard to take my eyes off her, so contrary to when I was a child and a young woman. I wished I didn't live so far away from her, so that I could pop in frequently.

Helen and Louise visited Hilda on my next visit to her. She seemed very pleased to see them and spent a few hours relating how she had been sexually abused by her step father when she was a little girl. Hence the reason she ran away from home. The girls found that part hard to listen to and it made them and me cry. She told us how when she was first pregnant with me, she told my father and he immediately left her and went back to his wife; we could not get any details of him, only that he was a "Very smart dapper man".

In those days there were no benefits of any kind and people had to work to provide for themselves. When she was ready to give birth to me she went into a nursing home and signed her step father's name on the bill and had it sent to him. He told the police and Hilda was taken into custody for two years because she was guilty of fraud. She said that I was taken away from her by the Social Services and she didn't see me for two years. When she came out of custody she moved me to a 'Baby Farm' which was apparently a notorious place to put children, they were not treated very well and they were very cheap. The term "Baby Farming" was common in the late 19th and early 20th Century cities, but by 1920 most places had taken action against the commercial practices and were on the decline. Most clients were unwed mothers. Although most Baby Farming amounted to what we now call family day care, they had terrible reputations. Stories were reported in newspapers which helped to mobilize political support for child welfare regulation and better standards. That was the reason that Nora decided she would look after me until Hilda got on her feet. Later Carol, Ruth, Charles, Jane and George all visited Hilda which she thoroughly enjoyed. Over the next few months I managed to visit many times, even though it was costly to get all the way to Portsmouth, how I wished she lived a little nearer.

CHAPTER 29

*H*elen found life hard without Derek and decided that she wanted to move on and move closer to Carol, who was living in the Wirral. This was a big blow for me, as I always seemed to lean on Helen in a crisis, and also regularly looked after George. We would miss having George, Karen and her around. I was very sad to see her move away from us to a house in Meols, Wirral, but nevertheless we wished her the best and hoped she would be very happy there.

For some time during 2002 and 2003 I felt that God was calling me to preach. What a disastrous situation, what did I know? I had been to church all these years but never really learned anything. After some soul searching and long talks with my friend Jane Parker, who encouraged me to believe what I was hearing, I told the minister (Andrew) that I wished to be a Local Preacher in the Methodist Church. He seemed very reluctant to accept this, but I soldiered on and went on 'Trial'. Yes, that is what they term a trainee preacher. After many months of study amounting to nearly four years and tearing my hair out with the studies, eventually I passed all the exams and was accepted as a Local Preacher in the Methodist Church in July 2007.

Charles and his girlfriend Sally had their first baby—Patrick Gabriel—at Fairfield Hospital on 1st April 2005. Patrick was a beautiful baby and everyone was delighted. Another grandchild! How fortunate we were to have such a lovely family.

My sister Valerie wrote to me every week and told me how much she loved me and wanted to see me. She had suffered a stroke when she was only 36 years old and had lost the use of one leg and arm. In spite of this she could produce some lovely embroidery. She sent me a cushion and a table cloth that she had embroidered for me. One day when we had driven down to Hilda's for a visit, we decided to call in at Valerie's on the way home. Valerie was delighted to see me and I was amazed at how like Ruth she looked. That was the last time I saw Valerie. It was a shame that we lived so far apart. Valerie died on Saturday 8th October 2005, two days after her 67th birthday. She had suffered a massive heart attack and was taken to The Hammersmith Hospital in London to the intensive care unit. She struggled to survive but eventually succumbed. I missed her writing me long letters, which always began with "My darling sister, Jen", which moved me almost to tears. Len was not keen on my going to the funeral, but I felt I should have done, because I needed to say goodbye to her. I felt very sad and also annoyed that I didn't share more time with her.

Charles announced he was to get married to Sally at last. The wedding would be on the 7th October 2006 and it was to take place at Egerton Hall Hotel, Bolton. We were really pleased for them both. The day came and we were entrusted with the care of Patrick for the night before and the special day. I found it hard to get myself ready as well as Patrick, so when Len was asking questions about his suit, etc., I told him I couldn't look or do anything about it as I was stressed out with my own jobs, thank you. Goodness knows what we both looked like, but Patrick looked really good! It was a lovely family day with all her family and ours. As Sally is the youngest of eight and Charles the youngest of five, the place was full of family members!

CHAPTER 30

*B*oth my knees were very painful to walk on so I was seen by an Orthopaedic Surgeon who advised me to have a complete knee replacement. I was certainly not keen to have this done, but walking would increasingly be more difficult without the operation.

I also had continual discomfort around the liver area and eventually was seen by a consultant at the Bupa hospital. After a scan and blood test, the Consultant conveyed the bad news that I had a stone in the gall-bladder which was attached to a polyp which was also in the gall bladder. He said that I must have an operation as soon as possible. The dilemma I was in was which operation to have first? Eventually I made up my mind to have the left knee replaced first. On the 4th January 2006 I went into hospital and had a knee replacement. The operation was a success and I did not have to have a full anaesthetic, I was given a spinal injection, which meant I was awake but sleepy.

Recuperation after a knee replacement is very slow and painful. I came home five days after the operation and my knee was so painful, I found it very difficult to sleep, even taking painkillers four times a day. On top of this I was to exercise every couple of hours. I did not enjoy being a patient,

I am much better as the nurse! The knee progressed very well, although it was extremely painful for three or four months. I managed with physiotherapy to get the knee bending at the rate which they said was right. The trouble was that the right knee also was painful and an X rayed showed that it was as bad as the left knee and would need to be operated on eventually. I had to push myself to move the knee and work hard to get it to bend properly. But after six months the knee was much less painful and I could bend it well. After this sort of operation sleep patterns seem to be altered and it was many months before I managed a good night's sleep.

April 2006 I went into the same hospital and had my gall bladder removed by keyhole surgery with a full anaesthetic. I recovered very well and settled down again to normal life; although the right knee stopped me walking very far due to considerable pain. The surgeon who had operated on the other knee advised me to have the right knee replaced as well. I didn't worry about the operation because I had already fared very well with the first one.

On 10th January 2007 I returned to the Bupa Hospital in Manchester for a complete knee replacement on the right knee. Again I had a spinal anaesthetic, but I cannot remember anything about the operation. I was extremely sick and felt very ill. They took some blood on the second day which showed a dramatic change in the liver function. All the chemicals were out of balance and some very high. They decided I had suffered Ischaemic Hepatitis. Apparently this is very rare, but when it happens 75% of patients die.

They assured me that the liver function tests would return to normal eventually, but until they did I would feel very sick and would need to rest. The cause of this liver problem was a sudden drop in blood pressure, but the reason for this was unclear. A liver scan and a cardiogram showed no problems, so we all agreed it would never be known what actually happened. I returned home after seven days in hospital and rested as much as I could.

A couple of days after I returned home from the hospital, in the night at 2.30am Len went to the toilet and collapsed on the bathroom floor. Needless to say I was totally unable to lift him up and he could not do it himself. I tried to get him to speak to me, but he did not reply; I was sure he had suffered a stroke or something just as terrible. How was I to get him over on to his back so that I could see what was the matter. As I was still on two crutches and still feeling very poorly, I realised I needed help. For the first time in my life I rang 999! The paramedics who came soon got him up off the bathroom floor and checked him over. They asked Len if he wanted to go into hospital, but he declined. He had a very high temperature and a chest infection and was probably not able to do anything for himself. I was devastated, as he was my full time carer. I rang Helen at 3.00am and told her, she immediately set off from her home to come to our aid. When she arrived after an awful journey in the fog, I was very weepy and sorry that I had called her, but she assured me that it was Ok and she and her boyfriend Graham stayed for the rest of the night and part of the next day to be sure that we were OK.

The rest of 2007 Len and I felt unwell some of the time and we then were persuaded to move nearer to Carol, Helen and Ruth. We put the bungalow on the market and proceeded to look for another house in and around Meols, Wirral. We eventually found a lovely apartment not far from the sea which suited us well and when the bungalow was sold we bought the apartment. Now would become another adventure in our partnership and it would be interesting how we took to living without a garden.

In February 2007 Helen married Graham who also had two children—Betty and Mandy.

On the 19th October we packed up and left Bury to move to the Wirral. The furniture went into storage for a few days while we stayed at Helen's house. Helen, Graham, Carol, Jim, Jane, Louise and Mike all came to decorate the flat before the carpets were laid. On the 24th we had the furniture out of storage and moved in. It was hard work, but very exciting. We could actually see the sea and Wales from the lounge window.

In December 2008 Sally and Charles had their second son, Joseph Nathaniel; another lovely grandchild.

CHAPTER 31

My brother James suddenly informed me that Hilda was now resident in a Nursing Home in Portsmouth and very poorly. I decided I must go and see her even though the distance was so great. Helen and I set off for Portsmouth at 8am and we arrived at James and Avril's house at 12.15pm. James and Avril had provided some sandwiches and we enjoyed being with them in their bungalow which had a lovely garden. James led the way to the Nursing Home in the afternoon and we saw Hilda. She was extremely ill and unable to speak. She nodded her head at us when James told her that Helen and I were there to see her. The whole visit was very traumatic, because Hilda was screaming out from time to time and it was difficult to tell if she was physically in pain or whether it was mental strain that caused her to make such loud noises. James was obviously very distressed, as were we. I sat with her for a while and thought about the past and whether all the screaming she was doing was due to the pain she had suffered in her life. How I wished we had more time to stay with each other, but I knew that she didn't have very long to stay. Sadly the time came for us to go, I kissed her and told her I loved her very much, she did answer me and say "I love you". Many tears were shed by all three of us, having to leave so soon. We left Portsmouth at about 4.15pm and Julie drove all the way home again. We had a very pleasant journey and talked about Hilda and the family all the way home. I was very grateful to Helen for giving up her time to accompany me.

Hilda died in April 2009, only a few days after our visit. Helen drove Len and me to Portsmouth for the funeral on 21st April 2009. It was a lovely sunny day. I was extremely nervous at being with all my half brothers and sisters at the same time; I was worried how they would receive me. Would they think I was after her things, or something? But it turned out very well, I was made very welcome. I was given a necklace belonging to Hilda, which I will keep forever. It was very sad to see all her worldly goods laid out on a small tray on a table.

Evelyn, the sister that I had not met was there and it was good to talk to her. I felt like I was looking at myself in a mirror when I looked at her. She was very tearful and upset about losing her mother, as were all of Hilda's children.

When we drove home, it seemed like the end of an era, and sad that I had had so little time to get to know them all. I know that James and Avril will keep in touch with me and I know that he loves me, because he keeps telling me so! How wonderful!

Do I regret not having more contact with Hilda, yes of course I do, but what we do in life depends on what is happening with other people as well as oneself? I can honestly say that I feel much less rejected and neglected, now that I have heard Hilda's story. It is so easy to know the answers after the event. My last memory of Hilda is seeing all my brothers and sisters at her funeral and each of us laying a red rose on her coffin as it was committed to the grave.

Now I had two mothers; I think about them both nearly every day. My life without either of them would be less happy.

On the 12th August 2009, Karen our granddaughter, and David her husband gave birth to Margaret Mia, our first **great** granddaughter, what a wonderful event for all of us.

So although my life has not ended yet, I feel it is important to make the most of any days we have. We both look forward with hope to more happy years together with our growing family.

Printed in Great Britain
by Amazon.co.uk, Ltd.,
Marston Gate.